THE **Biscuit Joiner**
PROJECT BOOK

Tips & techniques to simplify your woodworking using this great tool

JIM STACK

POPULAR
WOODWORKING
BOOKS

CINCINNATI, OHIO
www.popularwoodworking.com

READ THIS IMPORTANT SAFETY NOTICE

To prevent accidents, keep safety in mind while you work. Use the safety guards installed on power equipment; they are for your protection. When working on power equipment, keep fingers away from saw blades, wear safety goggles to prevent injuries from flying wood chips and sawdust, wear headphones to protect your hearing, and consider installing a dust vacuum to reduce the amount of airborne sawdust in your woodshop. Don't wear loose clothing, such as neckties or shirts with loose sleeves, or jewelry, such as rings, necklaces or bracelets, when working on power equipment. Tie back long hair to prevent it from getting caught in your equipment. People who are sensitive to certain chemicals should check the chemical content of any product before using it. The authors and editors who compiled this book have tried to make the contents as accurate and correct as possible. Plans, illustrations, photographs and text have been carefully checked. All instructions, plans and projects should be carefully read, studied and understood before beginning construction. Due to the variability of local conditions, construction materials, skill levels, etc., neither the author nor Popular Woodworking Books assumes any responsibility for any accidents, injuries, damages or other losses incurred resulting from the material presented in this book. Prices listed for supplies and equipment were current at the time of publication and are subject to change.

METRIC CONVERSION CHART

TO CONVERT	TO	MULTIPLY BY
Inches	Centimeters	2.54
Centimeters	Inches	0.4
Feet	Centimeters	30.5
Centimeters	Feet	0.03
Yards	Meters	0.9
Meters	Yards	1.1
Sq. Inches	Sq. Centimeters	6.45
Sq. Centimeters	Sq. Inches	0.16
Sq. Feet	Sq. Meters	0.09
Sq. Meters	Sq. Feet	10.8
Sq. Yards	Sq. Meters	0.8
Sq. Meters	Sq. Yards	1.2
Pounds	Kilograms	0.45
Kilograms	Pounds	2.2
Ounces	Grams	28.4
Grams	Ounces	0.04

Visit our Web site at www.popularwoodworking.com for more information and resources for woodworkers.

Other fine Popular Woodworking Books are available from your local bookstore or direct from the publisher.

07 06 05   6 5 4

Library of Congress Cataloging-in-Publication Data

Stack, Jim
   The biscuit joiner project book : tips and techniques to simplify your woodworking using this great tool / by Jim Stack.
     p. cm.
  ISBN 1-55870-592-9 (alk. paper)
  1. Woodworking tools. 2. Joinery. 3. Furniture making. I. Title.

TT186 .S73 2002
684'.083--dc21

2001036669

Edited by Jennifer Churchill
Designed by Brian Roeth
Lead photography by Al Parrish
Step-by-step photography by Jim Stack
Production coordinated by Sara Dumford
Editorial assistance by Megan Williamson
Technical illustrations by Melanie Powell, Studio in the Woods, mjp1@fast.net

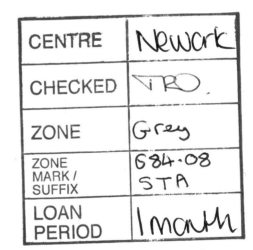
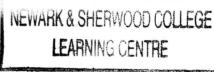

about the author

Jim Stack, the acquisitions editor for Popular Woodworking Books, is a cabinetmaker with 20-plus years of experience in commercial cabinetmaking shops. He loves to teach others about woodworking and believes the techniques you learn today should be passed on to others, who may improve upon those techniques tomorrow. Jim sincerely believes the satisfaction gained from sharing with others is what makes life worthwhile.

acknowledgements

I would like to thank Norma Petersen for allowing us to invade her home for four days while we photographed the projects in this book; Laura Robinson for her styling expertise; and Al Parrish for taking these truly gorgeous chapter opener photos.

As always, many thanks to Brian Roeth for his very creative design of this book. He certainly makes me look better than I am!

I am particularly grateful for the help of my good friend and editor, Jennifer Churchill, who continually goes above and beyond what is required. She made sense of all my words and thoughts.

I want to thank all the cabinetmakers and woodworkers I have worked with these past two decades. I know what I know and can do what I do because of their instruction and patience.

I dedicate this book to my wife and best friend, Gina. She has never wavered in her support of me and all my crazy ideas.

To my three children, who are now adults and still like to be around their Dad, I thank you for your never-ending friendship.

table of contents

WHITE OAK BOOKCASE

ASH ARMOIRE/MEDIA CENTER

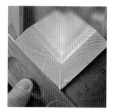

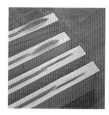

SYCAMORE CHEST OF DRAWERS

SMALL HANGING CUPBOARD

introduction

This book was a test to push the limits of the biscuit joiner. It did not fail anywhere.

In fact, it received extra credit for being so versatile and uncomplaining no matter what was asked of it. I don't claim to have learned all the tricks and uses of the biscuit joiner. This book is to be used merely as a jumping-off point for new uses of this amazing tool.

When I was starting out in the cabinetmaking business, the biscuit joiner wasn't anywhere to be seen. This tool was used in certain small circles that just didn't include commercial cabinetmaking shops. I don't remember the first time I used a biscuit joiner, but I do remember it was criticized as being a lazy and very questionable way to make joints, and that it probably wouldn't stand the test of use and time.

I had my own shop for several years, and I tried things that I wouldn't have been allowed to try while working for someone else. I used the biscuit joiner for several projects, and I was amazed at how easily and quickly the joint-making process became.

I remember making a small breakfast table for a client and assembling it using biscuits. It came apart at one of the leg joints, and I was very embarrassed, of course. I went to the client's house and put the table back together using the same biscuits in the same joint. I realized that I hadn't used enough glue to make the biscuits swell and make the joint tight. The table is still being used with no problems.

The last shop that I worked in used the biscuit joiner for a wide variety of applications, including large projects with large parts that wouldn't fit easily on our stationary power tools. So, we used the biscuit joiner instead, and simply took the tool to the project!

Some joints are left loose and unglued for installation purposes, such as large wall panels or cabinets that can't be built in one piece. Biscuits can serve as alignment guides in reassembling projects on-site. (The biscuit is glued in one side of the joint only.) One of the projects in this book is completely knockdown, and it's all done with the biscuit joiner.

You, the reader and woodworker, are invited to put the biscuit joiner to the test. You will think of new ways to use the tool, and it will make your woodworking even more fun, so now let's get to some projects!

biscuit joiner
BASICS

Few tools generate as much passionate debate as the biscuit joiner, arguably the most important woodworking tool invention in the last 50 years. Here, learn how to make your biscuit joints stronger, faster and more accurate.

by Christopher Schwarz

My first woodworking class years ago was all about hand-cut joints. We cut mortises, tenons, dovetails, half-laps, bridle joints — you name it. All with hand tools. It's a lucky thing a coping saw doesn't make much noise, because while cleaning out my 114th dovetail pin I overheard a classmate talking about biscuits.

Biscuits, he told us in hushed tones, are a faster and easier way to join wood. But some people, and he looked up at that moment to see if our instructor was listening, think that biscuits are cheating. Well, that was enough for me. I had to find out what all the fuss was about.

As it turns out, biscuit joinery is, in actuality, cheating — the same kind of way that nuclear weapons are cheating. Like 'em or not, they get the job done faster than anything else out there. Biscuits aren't right for every situation (chairs come quickly to mind), but for many projects, biscuit joints are just the thing.

First, they're strong. Lamello, the inventor of biscuit joinery, has done extensive stress testing on biscuit joints. In one of

Biscuit joiners cut a semicircular slot the perfect size for a biscuit — essentially a manufactured loose tenon. To illustrate how the machine works, we cut a slot in some Lexan, a tough polycarbonate plastic. Though this isn't a common application for the tool, it handled the job with surprising ease.

Where Do Biscuits Come From?

As important as the tool itself is the biscuit. These football-shaped pieces of wood are a bit of an engineering marvel. Out of the box, biscuits are about 0.15" thick, and they fit into a slot that's about 0.16". When the biscuit comes in contact with the water in your glue, it swells up, locking the joint in place. To ensure the joint is strong, the grain direction on biscuits runs diagonally. This prevents your joint from splitting and gives you, in the worst case, a cross-grained joint.

But just where do these little suckers come from? Kathleen Oberleiter, the dealer sales manager for Lamello, says her company has one plant in Switzerland that produces biscuits for Europe and the United States. In addition to producing biscuits under its own name, she says Lamello also makes the same quality biscuits for Makita and Black & Decker (and Black & Decker's sister company, DeWalt).

Lamello employs two people whose job is to find the perfect European beech trees for making biscuits. They look for trees that are at a particular stage of growth and choose those for harvesting. The trees are debarked, cut into thin panels and kiln dried. When the panels are dry, the biscuits are stamped and compressed from those panels. Lamello brags that all of its biscuits are within 0.1mm in thickness and with a moisture content between 8 and 10 percent.

Here in the United States, Porter-Cable started making its own biscuits in the mid-1980s in Jackson, Tennessee, according to company officials. Then the company decided it would be better to have another company make the biscuits using Porter-Cable's tooling and equipment. Now Hill Wood Products of Cook, Minnesota, makes all of Porter-Cable's biscuits. The company also makes Ryobi's face-frame biscuits. In fact, Hill Wood's plant is the only major producer of biscuits in this country and makes between 60 and 70 percent of the biscuits sold in the United States, says Hill Wood President Steve Hill.

Since his company started making biscuits for Porter-Cable, Hill says his company has upgraded the original equipment three or four times and can now easily make one million biscuits a day.

Instead of beech, Hill Wood makes biscuits using Northern white birch from Minnesota, most of which comes from within a 150-mile radius of the plant. The trees are sawn using special equipment and dried to a moisture content between 6 and 8 percent. Then the strips of birch are transformed into biscuits by the company's machinery.

Interestingly, Hill says Hill Wood does not compress the wood for its biscuits and relies on the moisture in the glue to swell the biscuit and lock the joint tight. The company's equipment is capable of compressing the biscuits, but Hill says he's found that wood can compress unevenly, resulting in biscuits of different thick-

Hermann Steiner, inventor of the Lamello biscuit joining system.

nesses. Hill Wood cuts its biscuits within 0.005" of the optimum thickness.

So how does birch compare to the European beech? Hill says beech is actually a little harder and the grain is a bit tighter than in birch, but that it's real close. "The glue or the wood is more likely to fail than the biscuit," he says.

Freud, a major player in the biscuit market, has its biscuits made by a Spanish firm that makes biscuits for many other firms, according to Jim Brewer, vice president of operations. Freud's biscuits are made of beech and are compressed, he says.

Biscuits sold by Ryobi are manufactured in Minnesota from beech and are compressed, company officials say.

Kaiser biscuits, which are made in Austria from beech, have been distributed in the United States for the last five or six years by Practical Products Company of Cincinnati, Ohio, according to Donald Baltzer, company president. Kaiser biscuits, which are respected in Europe, are compressed during manufacturing.

---

these tests, the scientists joined two pieces of beech end-grain to end-grain using a No. 20 biscuit. This was just about the weakest joint I could imagine. Then they had a machine grab each end and pull the joint apart. It took an average of 972 pounds of force to destroy it. Not bad for a little wafer of beech or birch.

Second, they're fast joints to make. We checked the amount of time it took to make several common joints for face frames. The winner was the pocket screw, but that's because there's no clamping time. Take out the clamping time, and biscuits and pocket screws tie for the fastest method.

Finally, biscuits are safe and easy to use. It's difficult to hurt yourself with a biscuit joiner; injuries are rare. In fact, I know of only two ways an injury could occur: The tool could slip or kick out of a cut and your left hand could get chewed up before the blade retracts, or you could plunge the biscuit joiner before you turn it on, in which case the tool would walk into the hand that's holding the piece and continue up your arm.

If you've never used a biscuit joiner, it will take you about five minutes to learn the basics. That said, there are some tricks to ensure your joints are perfectly lined up. Because the tool is so fast, it's easy to get lazy and a little sloppy.

The three most common sizes of biscuits: the No. 0 (the smallest), the No. 10 and the No. 20.

Biscuiting a Partition in the Middle of a Panel

Step 1 The best way to biscuit a partition into the middle of a panel is to use the partition itself as a fence for your biscuit joiner. Here's how: Mark on the panel where you want the partition to be placed.

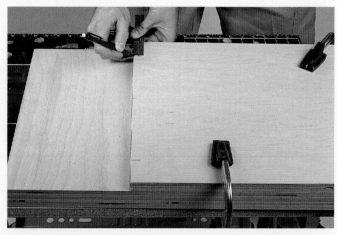

Step 2 Lay the partition flat on the panel and against the line you marked. Clamp the partition and panel to your bench. Mark where you want the biscuit slots to go; no need to mark the panel beneath it.

Step 3 Now remove the fence from your biscuit joiner. Place it flat on the panel and cut the slots in the partition.

Step 4 Now turn the biscuit joiner on its head and cut the slots in the panel. Use the layout lines on the partition and the centerline on the bottom of the tool to properly line up the biscuit joiner.

The Basic Basics

Biscuits can add strength to a joint, such as when you join a table apron to a leg. They can be used as an alignment aid when you edge-glue a panel using several boards or you need to edge-glue veneered panels. The biscuits won't add strength here, but they will keep your parts in line as you clamp. In a solid-wood panel, biscuits reduce the amount of time you spend leveling your joints. In veneered panels, biscuits keep your parts in line so you don't end up sanding through the veneer.

When making a biscuit joint, first put the two parts together and decide how many biscuits you need for that joint. A basic rule of thumb is to place your first bis-cuit 2" from the edge and then every 5" to 7" or so, though the spacing is really up to you. Draw a line across the joint at each spot where you want a biscuit. Set the fence on your biscuit joiner so the biscuit will be buried approximately in the middle of your material. For example, if you're working with ¾"-thick wood, set your biscuit joiner for a ⅜"-deep cut. Don't worry about being dead-on in the middle. If you cut all your joints from one side (say, the face side), everything will line up. Select the size bis-cuit you want to use and dial that into your tool. Use the biggest size you can.

Clamp one of your parts to your bench. Line up the line on the tool's fence or face-plate with the line on your work. Turn on the tool and allow it to get up to full speed. Plunge the tool into the wood and then out. Repeat this process for the other side of the joint.

Now glue up your joint. There are at least two ways of doing this. You can put glue in the slots and then insert the biscuit, or you can put glue on the biscuit and in-sert it in the slot.

For small projects, paint half the biscuit with glue and insert it into one of the slots. Then paint the other half of the biscuit and clamp your pieces together. This method produces clean joints with minimal squeeze-out, but it's a bit slow.

When assembling big projects, I like to put the glue in the slots first, using a bottle designed for this task. Squirt a dab of glue in all your slots and use a spare biscuit, a piece of scrap or a brush to paint the edges. Put the biscuits in the slots and clamp. The downside to this method is it's easy to use too much glue, and you're liable to get more squeeze-out.

No matter which method you use, be sure to go easy on the clamping pressure. It's easy to distort a frame made with biscuits. If you're using a regular yellow glue, clamp the project for at least 30 to 45 minutes before taking it out of the clamps.

Where to Use Biscuits

Making the biscuit slot is easy. The tricky part is knowing when to use biscuits and how many to use. Here are some situations when you should be careful.

LONG-GRAIN JOINTS: Many people use biscuits to join several narrow pieces into a panel, such as a tabletop. Biscuits help align the boards so they don't slip when you clamp them. However, don't let anyone tell you that the biscuits make the joint stronger. In long-grain to long-grain joints, the glue is stronger than the wood itself. So biscuits here are only an alignment tool. Also, be careful to place the biscuits where they won't show after you trim your part to finished size. Once I raised the panel on a door and exposed half a biscuit. That panel had to go in the trash.

FACE FRAMES: Biscuits are just right for face frames as long as your stock isn't too narrow. A No. 0 biscuit will work only with stock as narrow as $2\frac{3}{8}$". Any narrower and the biscuit will poke out the sides. To join narrow stock, you need a biscuit joiner that can use a smaller cutter or a tool that cuts slots for minibiscuits.

CONTINUOUS-STRESS JOINTS: Biscuits are strong, but I wouldn't build a kitchen chair with them. The joints in chairs, especially where the seat meets the back, are subject to enormous amounts of stress. Call me old-fashioned, but I'd use a mortise-and-tenon joint.

WITH POLYURETHANE ADHESIVES: We like poly glue quite a bit, but you must remember that biscuits swell and lock your joint in place by wicking up the water in your white or yellow glue. Poly glues have no moisture in them. In fact, these glues need moisture to cure. If you want to use poly glue with

Biscuiting an Apron to a Leg

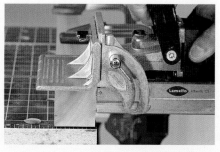

If you're going to use biscuits to attach a leg to a table apron, then you really should use two biscuits stacked on top of one another. This joint, according to experts and scientists, is nearly as strong as a mortise-and-tenon joint. The other challenge with this joint is you are going to want to offset the apron so it joins the middle of the leg. Here's the best way to do this: First determine what your offset is. I wanted my aprons to sit $\frac{1}{2}$" back from the legs. Now get a scrap piece of wood that is the same thickness as the offset. Put this block of wood on top of your apron and set the fence on your biscuit joiner to make the first cut. Make the cut on the apron.

Cut the biscuit slot on the leg without the spacer. When that's done, go back to your apron and adjust the fence to make the second biscuit slot.

Finally, cut the second row of slots on the leg without the spacer. When you're done, you've got a double helping of biscuits ready for some glue.

biscuits, dip your biscuits in water before inserting them into the slot. The water swells the biscuit and activates the poly glue.

BUILDING TABLES: If you're going to build a table using your biscuit joiner, use two stacked biscuits to attach the aprons and stretchers to the legs. This might mean making your aprons $\frac{7}{8}$" thick. (See the sidebar above for an easy way to get the apron in the right place and two biscuits into your joint.) In fact, whenever you're joining thick stock it's a good idea to add an extra biscuit.

ATTACHING A TABLETOP TO AN APRON
One of my favorite tricks with a biscuit joiner is using it to cut the slots for tabletop fasteners. Set the fence for $\frac{1}{2}$" (you want the slot to start $\frac{7}{16}$" down from the top of the apron) and make your cuts on the inside of the apron (you can do this after the table is assembled). The Z-shaped fasteners now slip into the slots and can be screwed to your tabletop.

WITH $\frac{1}{2}$" PLYWOOD: When using a biscuit joiner to join pieces of $\frac{1}{2}$"-thick plywood, you might have trouble with the biscuits "telegraphing" their shape into the surface of your material. Use No. 0 or No. 10 biscuits with $\frac{1}{2}$"-thick material and go a little easy on the glue.

Fence or No Fence?

Some woodworkers always rest the tool's fence on the work to control how deep the cut is; others prefer to take the fence off and let the tool's base ride on their bench or a

Biscuiting Miters

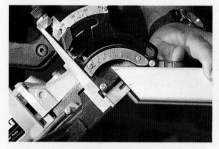

The fence on the Porter-Cable 557 allows you to biscuit your miters with the fence on the outside of the joint — a nice feature.

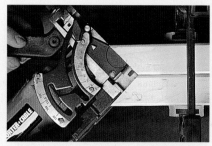

You can biscuit miters without using your fence by clamping the two joints together.

If your fence is adjustable only between 0° and 90°, you can cut the joint on the inside of the miter. Just be careful when positioning your tool.

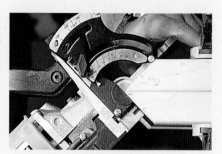

Or, if you have a fixed 90° fence on your tool, you can clamp them together this way to cut your slots.

table. Each approach has advantages. When you take the fence off and use your bench as the reference surface, you have a large flat area for your tool to rest against, and sniped boards won't throw off your joiner. However, you have to watch for sawdust and work with all your parts facedown on your bench. Advocates of the fence approach say it's easier and more accurate to work with your parts faceup on your bench. But you have to ensure your biscuit joiner is square to your work. If you lift up or press down on the tool during the cut, it could throw off your joint. Try each method and see which works best for you.

Quick Jig Speeds Your Work

There aren't a lot of jigs and fixtures for your biscuit joiner. However, building this jig will make the tool easier and safer to use. When I first started using biscuit joiners, I held the wood with my left hand and the tool with my right. After my grip failed me a couple times, I became an advocate of clamping your work in place.

But clamping takes time. This jig makes clamping quick and easy. The quick-release clamps allow you to fix your work in place in a second or two (with almost 300 pounds of clamping pressure), and it gives your biscuit joiner a bed to ride on.

Why is that important? You see, if you retract or remove the fence on your tool, the tool is designed to cut a slot in the middle of a ¾"-thick board when resting on a flat surface. So with this jig you don't need to set your fence. You simply clamp your wood in place, mark where you want the slot, put your tool on the bed and plunge.

This jig also makes your cuts more accurate because it ignores snipe on the ends of your stock. If you use the fence on your biscuit joiner when building face frames, you can get in trouble when the end of the

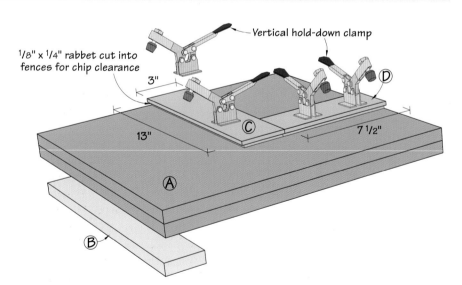

⅛" x ¼" rabbet cut into fences for chip clearance

Vertical hold-down clamp

3"

13"

7½"

Ⓐ Ⓑ Ⓒ Ⓓ

biscuit joinery clamping jig (inches)

NO.	LTR.	ITEM	DIMENSIONS T W L	MATERIAL
2	A	Beds	¾" x 18½" x 18½"	Ply
1	B	Cleat	¾" x 2½" x 18½"	Ply
1	C	Fence for stiles	½" x 3" x 13"	Ply
1	D	Fence for rails	½" x 3" x 7½"	Ply
1		Mitering guide	¾" x 8" x 15"	Ply

biscuit joinery clamping jig (millimeters)

NO.	LTR.	ITEM	DIMENSIONS T W L	MATERIAL
2	A	Bed	19 x 470 x 470	Ply
1	B	Cleat	19 x 64 x 470	Ply
1	C	Fence for stiles	13 x 76 x 330	Ply
1	D	Fence for rails	13 x 76 x 191	Ply
1		Mitering guide	19 x 203 x 381	Ply

4 De-Sta-Co clamps. Reid Tool Supply, 800-253-0421, www.reidtool.com, item #TC-215-U, $8.80 each.

Biscuit Joinery Clamping Jig

This jig is useful for two reasons. First, it will make your tool more accurate. You use the plywood base to guide your tool. That way if there's any snipe on the end of the board, your biscuit will still end up in exactly the right spot. Second, it will make your work a whole lot faster. The quick-release clamps on this jig (which supply hundreds of pounds of clamping force) let you work without clamping each piece to your bench, which slows you down. If you hold your face-frame parts down with your hand as you cut them, you'll find this jig is just as fast as that method, and your work is a lot less prone to slipping.

The beauty of this jig is that it holds both a rail and stile in place for cutting. You can cut one right after the other if you please, or cut them one at a time.

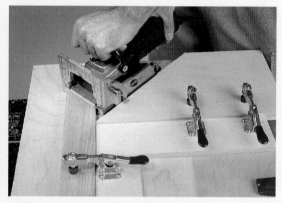

If you cut biscuits to join a mitered frame, this jig is quite useful when you add the 45° spacer shown in the photo. The spacer helps guide the tool and prevents it from kicking to the left, something that biscuit joiners are prone to do in narrow stock.

board is sniped. Because of the snipe, your tool won't cut the slot in the right place and your joints won't be flush.

With this jig, all you have to do is remember to put all your pieces facedown on the jig and keep it free of sawdust. Because the tool rides on the jig and not the work, your slot is going to be exactly where you need it.

I also made an attachment for this jig that guides the biscuit joiner when cutting slots in miters. This attachment keeps your tool on target and prevents it from kicking left as you plunge.

Building the jig takes less than 30 minutes. The most important part is the bed itself. You want it to be as flat as possible. Glue two pieces of ¾"-thick plywood together and check the "sandwich" for flatness with a straightedge. Then nail another piece of plywood on the bottom of the jig's front edge so the jig hooks over your bench.

Nail and glue two strips of ½"-thick plywood in the locations shown in the diagram on page 12. Then screw the clamps in place. Let the glue dry before you go to work; engaging the clamps at this point can tear your jig apart.

Troubleshooting

Not much goes wrong with biscuit joinery, but here are some of the troubles we've run into and how to remedy them.

Sometimes when you get in a hurry, your biscuit slots aren't aligned. The joint will either be whopper-jawed or impossible to clamp shut. Using a ruler, figure out which of the slots is off (it might be both). Glue a biscuit into the botched slot and let the glue dry. Then trim the biscuit flush to your material and cut your joint again.

When your biscuit joiner bogs down and burns the wood, it's trying to tell you something. Usually your blade is gummed up

with resin or it's dull. Remove the blade and spray it with an oven cleaner. If that doesn't help, have the blade sharpened.

Probably the weakest feature on most biscuit joiners is the dust collection. Typically, the tool tries to shoot the chips out a small port and into a cloth bag. This usually works for about half a dozen biscuits, then the port gets clogged and dust sprays everywhere when you make a slot. Sometimes this is a sign that your bag is getting old and frayed. The frayed ends cling together and the chips back up into the port and get clogged. If your bag is old, first try turning it inside out. If that doesn't help, just get an adapter to connect your tool to a shop vacuum. That will solve your problem.

AUTHOR'S NOTE: *Christopher Schwarz is senior editor for* Popular Woodworking *magazine. It is with his kind permission that this article is reprinted.*

small hanging
CUPBOARD

This small cupboard is a reproduction of an original Shaker design created in Mount Lebanon, New York, in the early 1800s. I scaled and detailed this piece using a photograph as my only guide. It has two adjustable shelves and would look good in any room in the house. This is a good first project; making it will give you the opportunity to learn and use fundamental biscuit joinery techniques. The original Shaker cupboard in the photograph was made of pine and had a warm brown color. This cabinet is made of sugar pine and finished with orange shellac. Then it was topcoated with precatalyzed lacquer to provide a water-resistant finish.

SMALL HANGING CUPBOARD *continued*

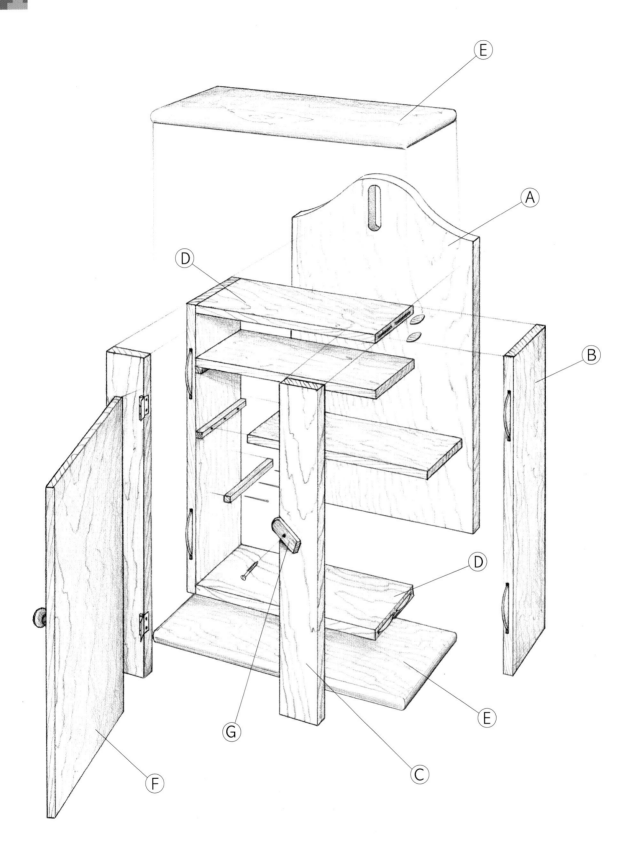

CUTTING LIST (INCHES) • small hanging cupboard

REF.	QTY.	PART	STOCK	THICKNESS	WIDTH	LENGTH	COMMENTS
A	1	Back	Sugar Pine	$1/2$	$11^1/2$	$16^1/2$	
B	2	Sides	Sugar Pine	$1/2$	$4^1/2$	13	
C	2	Fronts	Sugar Pine	$1/2$	2	13	
D	2	Top & Bottom	Sugar Pine	$1/2$	$4^1/2$	$10^1/2$	
E	2	Outer Top & Bottom	Sugar Pine	$1/2$	$5^3/4$	13	
F	1	Door	Sugar Pine	$1/2$	$7^1/2$	13	
G	1	Latch	Sugar Pine	$1/4$	$3/4$	$1^1/2$	

1 Pair Brass Hinges $3/8$" x 1"

CUTTING LIST (MILLIMETERS) • small hanging cupboard

REF.	QTY.	PART	STOCK	THICKNESS	WIDTH	LENGTH	COMMENTS
A	1	Back	Sugar Pine	13	292	419	
B	2	Sides	Sugar Pine	13	115	330	
C	2	Fronts	Sugar Pine	13	51	330	
D	2	Top & Bottom	Sugar Pine	13	115	267	
E	2	Outer Top & Bottom	Sugar Pine	13	146	330	
F	1	Door	Sugar Pine	13	191	330	
G	1	Latch	Sugar Pine	6	19	38	

1 Pair Brass Hinges 10mm x 25mm

Dipping Biscuits

When we started using the biscuit joiner in our cabinet shops about 10 years ago, I discovered it was much faster and more efficient to have a container of glue handy and simply dip the biscuits into it. After dipping, hold the biscuit over the slot and let a couple of drops fall into the slot. Then insert the biscuit and apply glue with a brush to the exposed part of the biscuit. On large jobs this process would speed up production, and my boss was very happy!

SMALL HANGING CUPBOARD *continued*

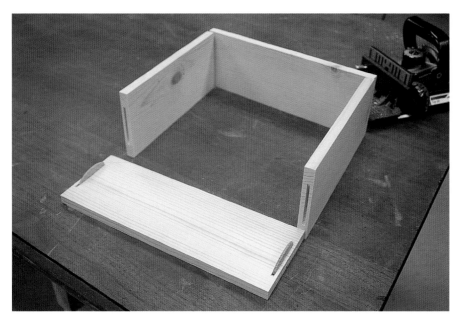

1 After cutting all parts to size, cut the slots for the ends and sides. Dry assemble the parts before gluing to be sure all the joints fit properly.

2 When clamping the sides and top and bottom together, be sure the assembly is square.

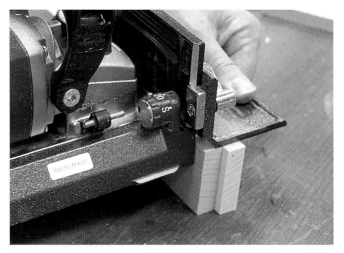

3 Here the slots are being cut into the two face panels. By laying the two parts on edge together, it's easier to hold the biscuit joiner square to the face of the panels.

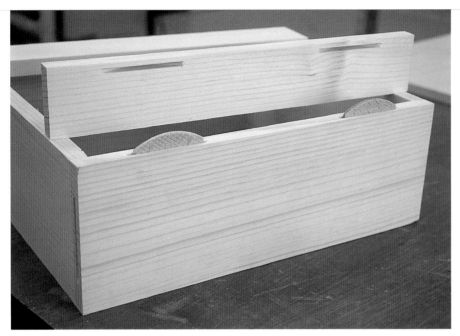

4 | Two biscuits will help align the panels with the cabinet sides.

5 | Be sure to use scrap pieces of wood between the clamps and the pieces being glued. This sugar pine is easily dented by the clamps.

6 | Attach the shelf brackets with small nails or brads. Use a spot of glue in the middle of the bracket if desired.

7 | Glue the top and bottom outer panels to the cabinet.

8 | To lay out the arch on the top of the back panel, first draw the center radius. Then, blend a second radius into the center radius to form a smooth transition. Cut and sand this curve smooth.

9 | Drill oversize screw holes (¼") in the back panel and attach it to the cabinet with screws. The oversize holes will let the back panel expand and contract with changes in humidity without cracking or splitting.

10 | The hinges are mortised into the door and screwed directly to the edges of the front panels.

Sizing Furniture

Sizing a piece of furniture from a photo is not difficult, but it does require a little imagination. If other objects (a glass or cup, a plate or potted plant) are in the photo, relative dimensions can be figured out by first measuring one of your own dishes. Then, using the same ruler you measured your plate with, measure the plate in the picture. These two measurements will give you an equation that says, for example, 1" = 10" (1" being the plate in the picture and 10" being the real plate). This equation will give you a scale to work with as you measure the piece of furniture in the picture. For example, if the furniture in the photo measures 2" across and $2\frac{3}{4}$" high, then by using the equation, you can figure that the piece is 20" across and $27\frac{1}{2}$" high ($\frac{1}{2}$ = 10/x and 1/2.75 = 10/x, where x = the full-size dimension). Many times I've been able to use an architect ruler, which has inches divided into increments that represent different lengths, so large objects can be drawn to a smaller scale and fit onto a piece of paper. Often a photo will be very close to one of the scales on this ruler.

If no other objects are in the photo except the piece of furniture, measure a similar piece of furniture that you have in your house and make an equation using the full-size measurement and the measurement you get from the photo. Tables, chairs, kitchen cabinets, book shelves, etc., all have standard heights and depths. These can help you determine dimensions in a photo.

After determining one dimension on the furniture in the photo (the top moulding, the width of a stile on a door or the height of a seat), you can figure out the rest of the measurements of the piece by visually getting a sense of these proportions as they relate to the whole piece. If you're interested in keeping the piece authentic, do some research about what kinds of woods and finishes were used at the time and place the piece was made.

curly maple
DESKTOP ORGANIZER

If you're like me, keeping things

organized is a challenge. This

project will help you create a place to

store a few things, therefore keeping your desktop

a little neater. This organizer is made of curly

maple, which makes the piece visual-

ly attractive. The basics of biscuit join-

ery are all that are needed to build this

project. The shelf unit is assembled with biscuits, as

is the drawer. Before final assembly, all the parts are

sanded and finished.

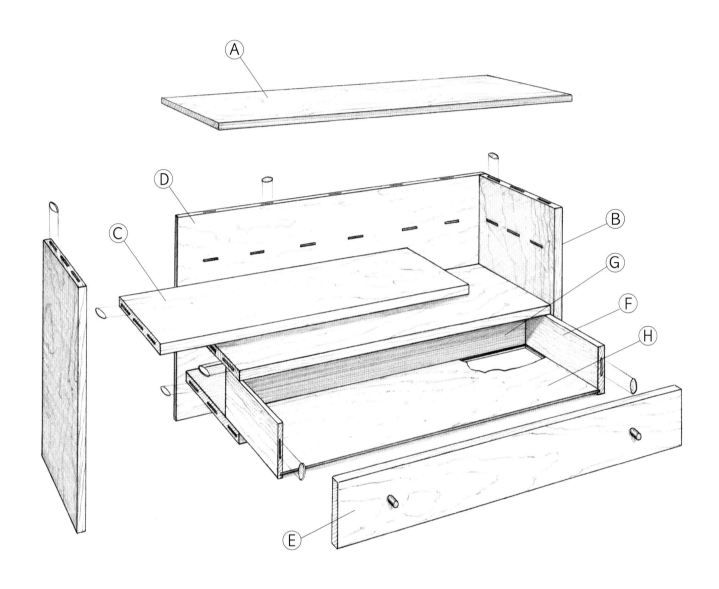

CUTTING LIST (INCHES) • curly maple desktop organizer

REF.	QTY.	PART	STOCK	THICKNESS	WIDTH	LENGTH	COMMENTS
A	1	Top	Curly Maple	$3/4$	10	30	
B	2	Sides	Curly Maple	$3/4$	$9^3/4$	$17^1/4$	
C	3	Shelves	Curly Maple	$3/4$	$8^3/4$	$26^1/2$	
D	1	Back	Birch Ply	$3/4$	$14^1/4$	$27^1/2$	
E	1	Drawer Front	Curly Maple	$3/4$	3	$26^1/2$	
F	2	Drawer Sides	Maple	$1/2$	3	$7^3/4$	
G	1	Drawer Back	Maple	$1/2$	$2^1/4$	$25^1/2$	
H	1	Drawer Bottom	Luan Ply	$1/4$	8	26	
J	2	Pulls	Oak Dowel	$3/4$ diameter		1	

CUTTING LIST (MILLIMETERS) • curly maple desktop organizer

REF.	QTY.	PART	STOCK	THICKNESS	WIDTH	LENGTH	COMMENTS
A	1	Top	Curly Maple	19	254	762	
B	2	Sides	Curly Maple	19	248	438	
C	3	Shelves	Curly Maple	19	222	673	
D	1	Back	Birch Ply	19	362	699	
E	1	Drawer Front	Curly Maple	19	76	673	
F	2	Drawer Sides	Maple	13	76	197	
G	1	Drawer Back	Maple	13	57	648	
H	1	Drawer Bottom	Luan Ply	6	203	660	
J	2	Pulls	Oak Dowel	19 diameter		25	

2 | CURLY MAPLE DESKTOP ORGANIZER *continued*

1 | Lay the two side panels side by side and cut all the biscuit slots at the same time. This will ensure that the shelves will be level and the project will be square when assembled.

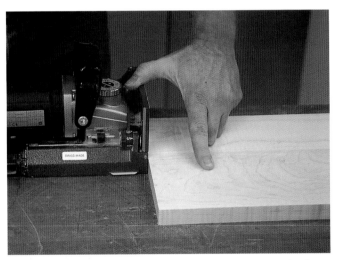

2 | Lay the shelves faceup on a flat surface when cutting the slots. The bottoms of the shelves will then be located correctly with the slots that have been cut in the sides.

3 | Stand the top on its back edge and cut the slots that line up with the back panel. Next, cut the slots in the top where the sides will attach to the top, using the layout square. To locate the slots, dry assemble the base of the project and measure the distance between the slots in the tops of the sides. Transfer this measurement to the top panel, making sure the top will be centered on the base.

4 After the slots have been cut and you've determined that the parts fit together properly, finish sand all the parts. Cover the slots with masking tape, and finish the parts.

5 To keep the finish out of the slots, cover them with tape.

6 Let the finish cure overnight, then assemble the project. (You will find it easier to clean up any glue that oozes out of the joints, because the unit was finished prior to assembly.)

7 The back is screwed to the base. Note that the screw is inserted at a slight angle so it won't cause a bulge on the inside of the project.

8 Glue the top in place.

9 Detail of drawer and white oak ¾" dowel pull. Any wooden dowel would make a nice, simple pull for the drawer. For construction details of the drawer, see the sidebar "Making a Drawer Using Biscuit Joinery."

Making a Drawer Using Biscuit Joinery

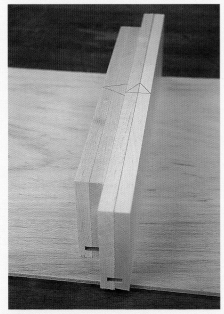

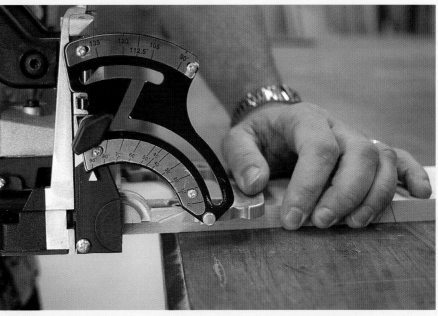

Step 1 Lay out all the drawer parts in order, and label using an orienting triangle. Remember that the drawer sides will capture the front and back when the drawer is assembled.

Step 2 Mark the location of the biscuits and cut the slots in the front and back parts. When making drawers, use the largest biscuits you can.

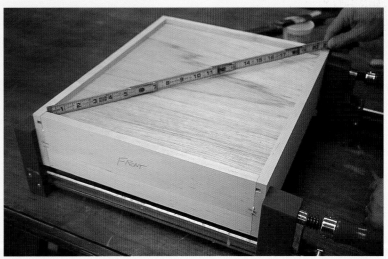

Step 4 Assemble the drawer. You can either use a captured bottom (as shown here) or cut the bottom of the back part off. The bottom can then be slid into the assembled drawer after the drawer and bottom have been finished.

Step 3 Cut the slots into the sides.

curved-leg
NIGHTSTAND

When I was teaching a woodworking class, I needed a project

that would show the students how the woodworking process

worked, from design to finish. This table design was a

result of that class. The original table was rec-

tangular and had a drawer at one end. The join-

ery at the legs and aprons is different from the

joinery on a standard table; the legs are set at 45° angles to

the aprons. This joinery is made-to-order for biscuit assembly.

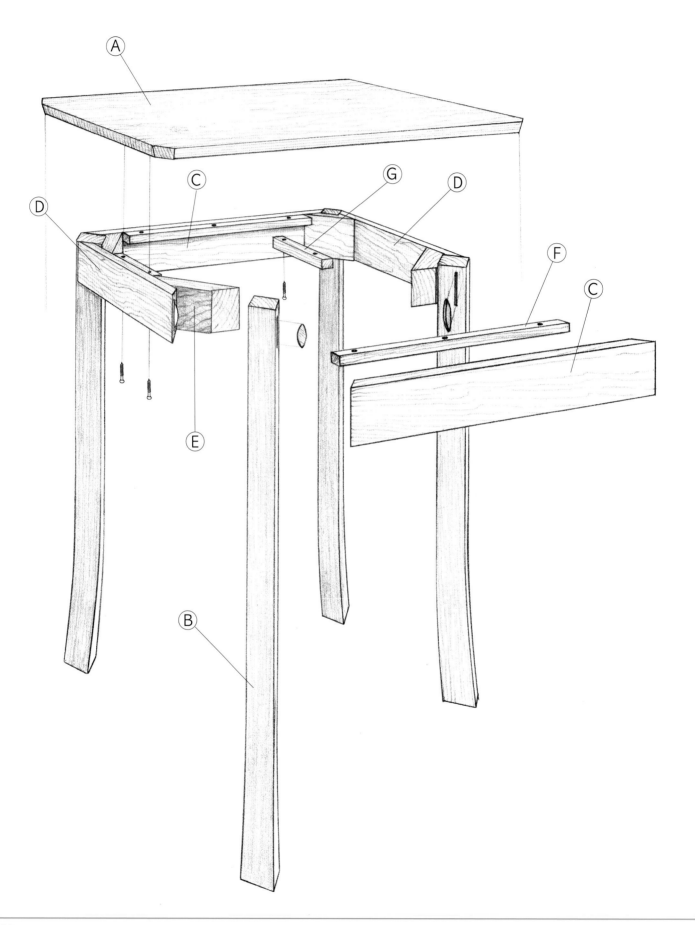

CUTTING LIST (INCHES) • curved-leg nightstand

REF.	QTY.	PART	STOCK	THICKNESS	WIDTH	LENGTH	COMMENTS
A	1	Top	White Oak	1	$17^{1}/_{2}$	$20^{1}/_{4}$	
B	4	Legs	White Oak	$1^{1}/_{4} - 1^{3}/_{4}$	$1^{1}/_{4}$	$24^{1}/_{2}$	
C	2	Aprons	White Oak	$3/_{4}$	$2^{1}/_{2}$	17	
D	2	Aprons	White Oak	$3/_{4}$	$2^{1}/_{2}$	$14^{3}/_{8}$	
E	4	Corner Blocks	White Oak	$1^{1}/_{4}$	2	$3^{7}/_{8}$	
F	2	Cleats	White Oak	$3/_{4}$	$3/_{4}$	12	
G	2	Cleats	White Oak	$3/_{4}$	$3/_{4}$	9	
H	12	No. 8 x $1^{1}/_{4}$" Flathead Screws					

CUTTING LIST (MILLIMETERS) • curved-leg nightstand

REF.	QTY.	PART	STOCK	THICKNESS	WIDTH	LENGTH	COMMENTS
A	1	Top	White Oak	25	445	514	
B	4	Legs	White Oak	32–45	31	623	
C	2	Aprons	White Oak	19	64	432	
D	2	Aprons	White Oak	19	64	366	
E	4	Corner Blocks	White Oak	31	51	98	
F	2	Cleats	White Oak	19	19	305	
G	2	Cleats	White Oak	19	19	229	
H	12	No. 8 x 32mm Flathead Screws					

Making a Tapering Jig

1 | Cut strips for the table legs using a tapering jig (see sidebar "Making a Tapering Jig"). Six strips are needed for each leg.

Step 1 Square a long block of solid wood or laminate some plywood pieces together to create a thickness of $1\frac{1}{2}$". The taper for the side table strips will be $\frac{1}{16}$"–$\frac{1}{8}$". (The greater the taper, the larger the flare will be at the bottom of the legs.) Draw the taper on the wood blank and cut it with a jigsaw or a band saw or hand-plane it.

Step 2 Attach a plate to the top of the jig. This will hold the strips of wood in place as you are cutting them. This is a very important safety factor: The plate will protect your fingers from the saw blade, and the wood strip won't be pulled into the blade and cause a kickback. Keep the strips in order as you cut them, so that when they are glued back together, the grain will closely match the original piece of stock they were cut from. The photo here shows the jig upside-down.

2 | Apply glue to the strips and clamp them together using a simple bending form (see sidebar "Making a Bending Form" on page 37). Note the use of a $\frac{1}{4}$"-thick strip of wood to protect the laminations and to even out the clamping pressure.

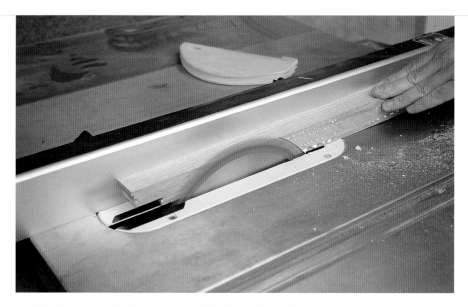

3 After the legs have been glued, plane or joint the laminations level on one edge. Plane or cut (using the table saw) the legs to thickness.

4 Cut the legs to length on the table saw. Next, cut the aprons to length with a 45° cut on each end.

5 Cut the biscuit slots in the legs.

6 Cut the biscuit slots in the ends of the aprons.

7 | Assemble the table. Note the clamping blocks with wedge cuts. These blocks protect the apron pieces plus create an easy way to clamp the whole assembly together.

8 | Cut the bevels on the edges of the top.

9 | Cut the bevels on the corners of the top.

10 | Glue the corner blocks in place. Then glue the cleats to the aprons. Drill oversize holes in the cleats and attach the top with screws. The oversize holes allow the screws to move with the solid-wood top as it expands and contracts; this prevents it from cracking or splitting.

Making a Bending Form

A one-piece bending form is a simple, yet effective way to laminate strips of wood to create any curve. Forms can be made from scrap wood, preferably plywood, because it is stable and strong. If the form needs to be thicker than the scraps you have, simply glue pieces to the thickness you need. Draw the pattern you would like on the blank you've made. Cut next to the pattern line with a jigsaw or band saw and sand or plane the curve smooth to the line. Wax the edges of the form where the lamination strips will be against it, so no squeezed-out glue will stick the laminated piece to the jig.

Lamination bending of wood is good for several reasons; one is that wood has a memory, and it will try to return to its original shape if it's steam bent. Strength is another reason to consider doing lamination bending. When wood is steam bent, the fibers are stretched and sometimes fracture. This weakens the wood. However, if wood is cut into narrow strips, it can be easily bent, and very little stress is placed on the wood fibers. Once the glue has set up (usually 2 hours), there is no springing back of the laminated wood piece, and it is very strong.

The downside to lamination bending is that when the wood is cut into strips, a lot of the wood becomes sawdust, but if you select your wood with this waste factor in mind, it is worth buying a little extra so you can create some beautiful bent shapes.

showcase cherry
WALL CABINET

Making this cabinet will give you experience

assembling a larger, more difficult project.

The cherry wood, glass panels in the doors, bevel

on the edges of the bottom, and crown moulding on the top

give this cabinet a formal appearance. The following alterations

would make this cabinet a good choice for installing in a kitchen

or pantry: Change the wood to red oak or birch, use wood pan-

els in the doors, cut the bottom edges square and keep the top

flat, or fit it next to the ceiling.

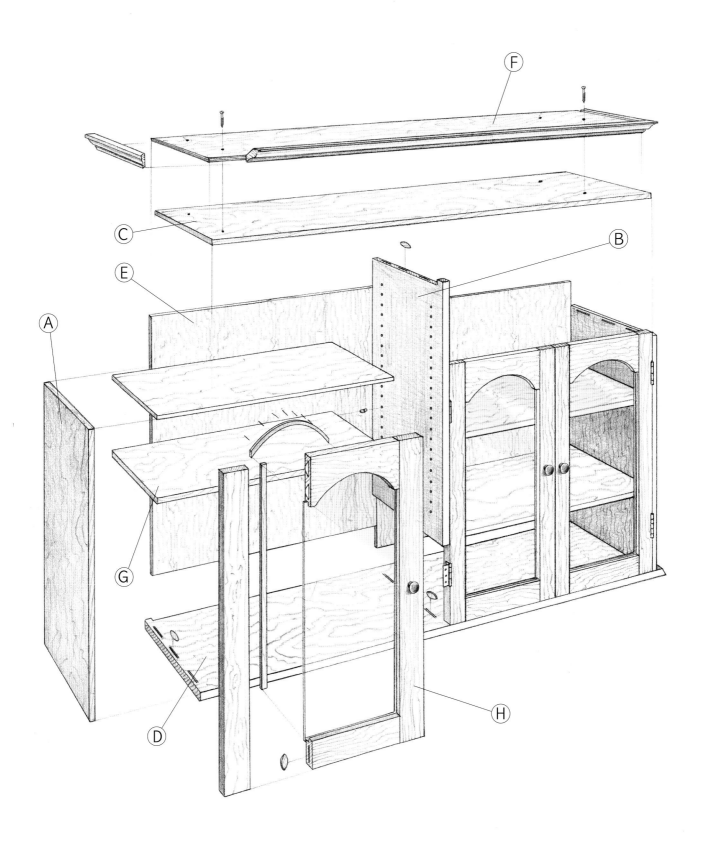

CUTTING LIST (INCHES) • showcase cherry wall cabinet

REF.	QTY.	PART	STOCK	THICKNESS	WIDTH	LENGTH	COMMENTS
A	2	Ends	Cherry	$3/4$	$12^5/8$	$31^1/4$	
B	1	Partition	Cherry	$3/4$	$12^1/8$	$31^1/4$	
C	1	Top	Cherry	$3/4$	$11^1/4$	$68^1/8$	
D	1	Bottom	Cherry	$3/4$	$13^1/2$	$71^3/8$	
E	1	Back	Cherry	$1/2$	$31^5/8$	$69^1/8$	
F	1	Top Plate	Cherry	$1/2$	$12^1/2$	$69^1/2$	
G	4	Shelves	Cherry	$3/4$	$11^1/4$	$33^5/8$	
H	4	Doors	Cherry	$7/8$	$16^3/4$	$31^1/8$	
J	10'	Crown Moulding	Cherry	$3/4$	$3^1/4$		
DOOR PARTS	8	Stiles	Cherry	$7/8$	$2^1/4$	$31^1/8$	
	4	Top Rails	Cherry	$7/8$	5	$12^1/4$	
	4	Bottom Rails	Cherry	$7/8$	$2^1/4$	$12^1/4$	
	16	Shelf Pins					
	4 Sets	$1^1/4$" x 2" Brass Butt Hinges					
	4	Knobs					

CUTTING LIST (MILLIMETERS) • showcase cherry wall cabinet

REF.	QTY.	PART	STOCK	THICKNESS	WIDTH	LENGTH	COMMENTS
A	2	Ends	Cherry	19	321	793	
B	1	Partition	Cherry	19	308	793	
C	1	Top	Cherry	19	285	1730	
D	1	Bottom	Cherry	19	343	1813	
E	1	Back	Cherry	13	803	1756	
F	1	Top Plate	Cherry	13	318	1766	
G	4	Shelves	Cherry	19	285	854	
H	4	Doors	Cherry	22	425	790	
J	3050mm	Crown Moulding	Cherry	19	82		
DOOR PARTS	8	Stiles	Cherry	22	57	790	
	4	Top Rails	Cherry	22	127	311	
	4	Bottom Rails	Cherry	22	57	311	
	16	Shelf Pins					
	4 Sets	32mm x 51mm Brass Butt Hinges					
	4	Knobs					

SHOWCASE CHERRY WALL CABINET *continued*

1 | Cut the bevels on the bottom panel using the table saw.

2 | The front edge of the center partition continues over the front edge of the top. I glued a strip to the front of the partition to create the offset, but it also could be made by cutting a notch at the top of the panel.

3 | Use a layout square (see sidebar "Making a Layout Square") as a guide for cutting the biscuit slots in the bottom panel. Note that the layout square is aligned with the end of the top panel. (The top panel has been centered and set against the edge of the bottom panel so that the layout for all the vertical panels will be perfectly aligned on both panels at the same time.) This is the point where the side panel will be located on the bottom panel. By cutting the slots on the outside of the layout square, the biscuits will be positioned properly.

Making a Layout Square

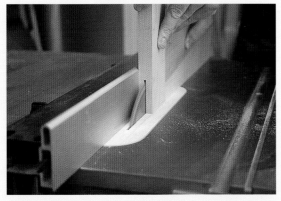

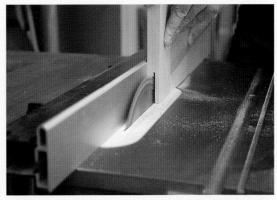

Step 1 After cutting the parts to size, cut a slot into the end of the wooden arm. Make the first cut just off center. Note the square scrap of wood being used as a push stick. This scrap helps you to hold the wood squarely to the table and protects your fingers from the blade as it exits the back of the cut.

Step 2 Turn the piece around and make the second cut. Test fit the plastic arm, and adjust the saw fence if necessary to make the slot the proper size. Use this same procedure to cut the slot in the other end of the wooden arm for the small plastic leveling piece.

Step 4 Set the layout square against a flat edge and draw a line as shown.

Step 3 Lay the parts out on a flat surface. Install the leveling piece into one end of the wooden arm with two countersunk screws. Use a framing square to help hold the two arms at right angles to each other. Insert only one screw and tighten it snugly.

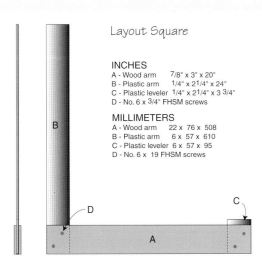

Layout Square

INCHES
A - Wood arm   7/8" x 3" x 20"
B - Plastic arm   1/4" x 21/4" x 24"
C - Plastic leveler 1/4" x 21/4" x 3 3/4"
D - No. 6 x 3/4" FHSM screws

MILLIMETERS
A - Wood arm   22 x 76 x 508
B - Plastic arm   6 x 57 x 610
C - Plastic leveler 6 x 57 x 95
D - No. 6 x 19 FHSM screws

Step 5 Flip the square over and check it against the line you just drew. The line should line up with the square. If it doesn't, adjust the square (you've got only one screw installed, so this is easy). Repeat this process until the layout square is as accurate as you can make it. Install the other screws; two on one side at diagonals to each other, and two on the other side at opposite diagonals. This will hold the square firmly at a right angle. I've made a lot of these squares, and even if they fall on the floor, they stay true!

5 | Mark all of the parts to indicate which way they will be configured when the cabinet is assembled. This photo shows the two end panels labeled and the rabbet cuts drawn out so there is no mistaking where the machining needs to be done.

4 | Cut the slots for the partition biscuits in the center of the top and bottom panels.

7 | Cut the rabbet in the back edge of the bottom panel with a rabbeting bit and a router. Stop the cut at both ends of the bottom panel, and square the rabbet at each end using a chisel.

6 | The rabbets in the end panels can be cut using the jointer or the table saw.

Tip *Slowly backing the router into the cross grain will eliminate wood tear-out. (Take small cuts when backing the router into a cut.) Finish the cut, pushing the router the correct direction.*

8 | Glue the end panels to the top panel. Note that the center panel is being used as a support for the top panel. This helps keep the top panel flat and ensures that the end panels will be square to the top panel.

10 | The back of the cabinet is in two pieces because the grain runs vertically. This was the only way to cut it out of a 4×8 sheet of ½" plywood. If you choose to have the grain run horizontally, the panel could then be cut out in one piece.

9 | Glue the center panel to both the top and bottom panels at the same time that you glue the bottom panel to the end panels. As you clamp the assembly together, check to be sure it is square.

11 Use the table saw to cut the crown moulding. Set the miter gauge to 45°. Hold the face of the moulding toward the fence with the bottom edge of the moulding flat on the table saw, and make the cut.

12 To cut the opposite corner, reverse the 45° setting on the miter gauge. Put the gauge in the slot on the other side of the blade, and make the miter cut on the opposite end of the long crown moulding piece. You get perfectly cut miters every time!

13 Glue the long crown moulding to the ½" plywood top mounting plate. Note that a hand screw is used to hold the mounting plate vertical. (It's like having an extra set of hands.)

14 | Draw the door top-rail arch on a piece of scrap plywood. Cut next to the line, and smooth to the line with files and sandpaper. This will be your template, so take your time and make it as smooth as you can. Trace the arch onto each rail. Cut on the inside of the arch lines leaving about ⅛" of material. Set up the routing jig as shown in the photo, and rout each rail arch with a flush-trim bit in the router. If you rout with a sharp bit, the edge will require very little sanding.

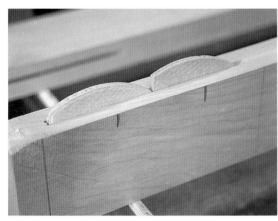

15 | When cutting the slots for this joint, overlap them just a little. Two No. 20 biscuits will fit tightly end to end into the top rails of the doors. Note that one of the biscuits has been trimmed. This is perfectly acceptable and doesn't affect the strength of the joint.

16 | After the glue has cured, rout the rabbet for the glass using a rabbeting bit in a router. Square the corners of the rabbet with a chisel.

Making a Butt Hinge Routing Jig

In a piece of scrap ¼" plywood, cut a notch the length of the hinge plus the width of the router base minus the diameter of the router bit. Got that? OK. The depth of the notch is the width of one hinge leaf plus the distance from the outside of the router bit to the back edge of the router base.

Clamp two strips of wood flush to the edge of the door and mount the plywood template to these two scraps as shown in the photo. Make as many test cuts as you need to get the mortise correct. Once you have it set up, it will cut hundreds of mortises, each one exactly the same as the other.

17 | Brass butt hinges are used to hang the doors. This photo shows a simple but effective jig for cutting the mortises for the butt hinges (see the sidebar "Making a Butt Hinge Routing Jig"). Square out the corners of the mortise with a chisel. Cutting one of these mortises takes about 2 minutes, from clamping the jig setup to the door, to the squaring of the mortise corners.

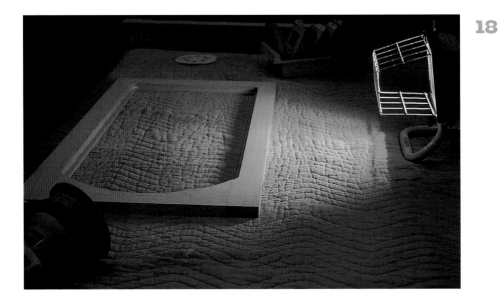

18 | Use a task light to cast a sharp light across the surface of the wood while you are finish sanding. The light will show any imperfections you need to sand out to make the surface smooth.

19 | The glass in the doors is held in place with cleats that fit into the rabbet. The curved cleats are made by milling wood stock to the same thickness as the straight cleats. Set up a sled on the band saw that pivots on a center that is perpendicular to the band saw blade. The pivot is set to the radius (the distance from the blade to the pivot) of the inside of the rabbet in the arch of the door. Cut curved strips from the wood blanks, leaving extra material for cutting to final width.

20 | After the oversize strips are cut, set up a stop on the inside of the band saw blade. The distance between the stop and the blade is equal to the width of the straight glass cleats. Hold the outside of the curved cleat against the stop and cut the cleat to finished width. Sand the cleats smooth and finish. Trim them to length as needed and install with small brads.

21 | Use a shelf-pin hole drilling template to bore the holes for the shelf pins.

Making a Shelf-Pin Hole Drilling Template

Make the template from a scrap piece of plywood. Mark where to drill the holes on the plywood at 1$\frac{1}{4}$" (or 32mm) on center and use a drill press to bore the holes. (I prefer 5mm diameter holes because I think they look better than a larger $\frac{1}{4}$" hole.) This will give you a cleanly cut, straight hole.

Be sure to clearly mark the template's bottom, top, inside and front. Do this on both sides of the template, as you will reverse it when drilling holes in the left and right sides of a cabinet. The markings will ensure that all of the holes will line up on both sides of the cabinet and also will keep you from getting the template reversed or flipped upside down.

Another method is to use a piece of $\frac{1}{4}$" perforated hardboard (Masonite). The holes are 1" apart on center, and you will need a $\frac{1}{4}$"-diameter (6mm-diameter) drill bit to bore the shelf-pin holes.

white oak
BOOKCASE

This project is based on actual plans for a Craftsman bookcase.

The original has tenons on its shelves that go through the sides

and are held in place with wedges inserted into the

ends of the tenons. I maintained the shape, dimen-

sions and hardware that appeared on the original

plans. Using biscuits, this bookcase was much

easier to make — and it looks great. I

used a clear finish on the white oak,

rather than using traditional Arts-and-

Crafts fumed, dark, oak staining. The wood will eventually devel-

op a beautiful golden-brown patina.

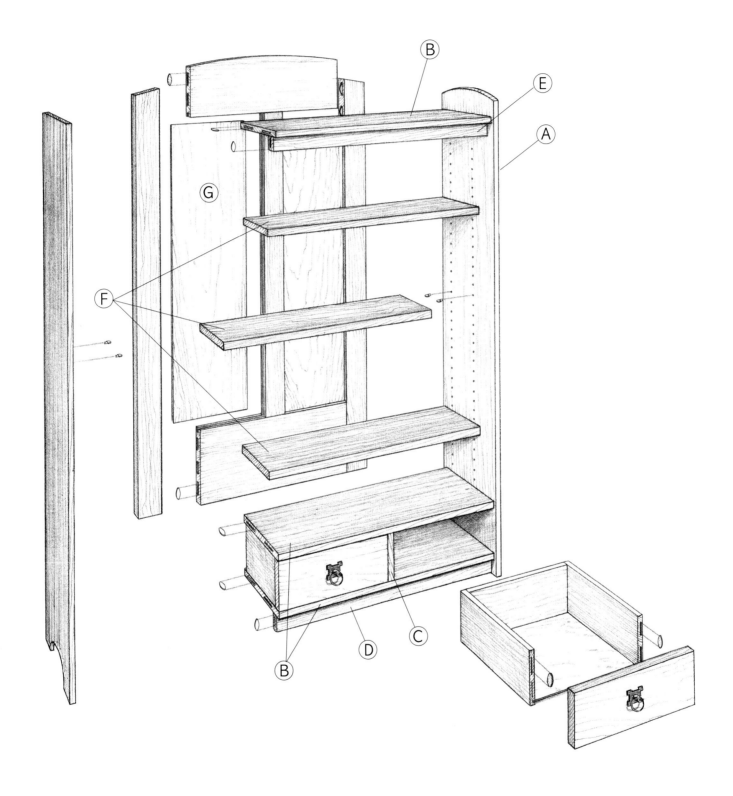

CUTTING LIST (INCHES) • white oak bookcase

REF.	QTY.	PART	STOCK	THICKNESS	WIDTH	LENGTH	COMMENTS
A	2	Ends	QSWO*	$3/4$	14	66	*QSWO = Quartersawn white oak
B	3	Top & Two Bottoms	QSWO	$3/4$	13	$34^{1}/_{2}$	
C	1	Center Divider	QSWO	$3/4$	6	$12^{7}/_{8}$	
D	1	Kick Plate	QSWO	$3/4$	2	$34^{1}/_{2}$	
E	1	Top Shelf Rail	QSWO	$3/4$	$1^{1}/_{2}$	$34^{1}/_{2}$	
F	3	Adjustable Shelves	QSWO	$3/4$	10	$34^{1}/_{2}$	
G	1	Back	QSWO	$3/4$	$34^{1}/_{2}$	65	
BACK PARTS	3	Stiles	QSWO	$3/4$	4	46	
BACK PARTS	1	Crest Rail	QSWO	$3/4$	7	$34^{1}/_{2}$	
BACK PARTS	1	Bottom Rail	QSWO	$3/4$	12	$34^{1}/_{2}$	
BACK PARTS	2	Panels	QSWO	$1/4$	$12^{1}/_{4}$	47	Panels are resawn and bookmatched
	12	Shelf Pins					

CUTTING LIST (MILLIMETERS) • white oak bookcase

REF.	QTY.	PART	STOCK	THICKNESS	WIDTH	LENGTH	COMMENTS
A	2	Ends	QSWO*	19	356	1676	*QSWO = Quartersawn white oak
B	3	Top & Two Bottoms	QSWO	19	330	877	
C	1	Center Divider	QSWO	19	152	327	
D	1	Kick Plate	QSWO	19	51	877	
E	1	Top Shelf Rail	QSWO	19	38	877	
F	3	Adjustable Shelves	QSWO	19	254	877	
G	1	Back	QSWO	19	877	1651	
BACK PARTS	3	Stiles	QSWO	19	102	1168	
BACK PARTS	1	Crest Rail	QSWO	19	178	877	
BACK PARTS	1	Bottom Rail	QSWO	19	305	877	
BACK PARTS	2	Panels	QSWO	6	311	1194	Panels are resawn and bookmatched
	12	Shelf Pins					

1 After cutting all the parts, lay out the sides next to each other so it is clear to you which will be left and right. Use a set of trammel points to draw the arc at the tops of the sides. Bending a thin strip of wood to the desired arc will also work.

2 | At the bottom of the sides, mark where the feet will be and draw these vertical lines using a square held against the bottom of the side panels. Mark how far up the cutout will go, and mark that square to the sides. Then draw another line parallel to this line ¼" below it. Use a cup or small can and draw an arc connecting the vertical lines with the lower horizontal line. Bend a thin strip of wood (or a small-diameter wooden dowel rod) connecting the small arcs with the top horizontal line at its center. Have an assistant draw this arc. This is a simple way to connect differing arcs to form a pleasing overall shape.

3 | Mark the arc on the crest rail as shown. Mark on both ends of the rail how far down you would like the arc to go. Put a mark at the center top of the rail, and connect the dots as shown.

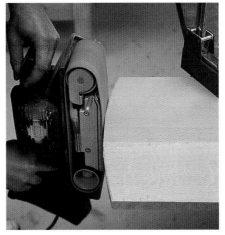

4 | Rough-cut the top arcs, and smooth with a belt sander or by hand with a sanding block.

5 | You could also make a template and rout the arcs. This ensures that both sides will be the same, and it also makes the final edge cleanup easier.

6 | Cut the bottom arcs and sand smooth, or make a template and rout the cutouts.

Tip *Sometimes mistakes happen! I had the biscuit joiner set to make a deep plunge cut using the smaller cutter. When I changed back to the standard cutter, I forgot to change the depth-of-cut setting. The first cut I made went all the way though the side panel on the bookcase. To patch the slot, I cut a piece of cross-grained scrap to fit into the slot and glued it in place (see Photo 1). The patch blended very well with the surrounding grain pattern (see Photo 2).*

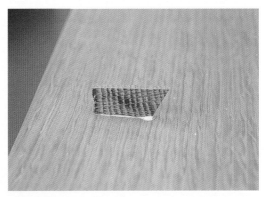

Photo 1

Photo 2

7 | This common trick for cutting biscuit slots in the edge of one part and the flat of another is very accurate and easy to do (see the sidebar "Biscuiting a Partition in the Middle of a Panel" on page 10). Cut the first set of slots.

8 | Turn the router around and cut the second set of slots.

9 | Draw a line parallel to and ⅜" from the front edge of both the top and bottom panels. Glue the kick rail and top rail in place, using the lines as your reference.

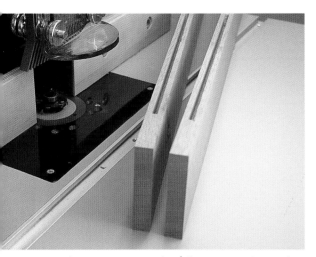

10 | A router set up with a ¼" wing cutter is a good way to make the stopped grooves in the back panel rails and stiles.

11 | Before assembling the back panel, finish sand the ¼" panels. After the back panel is assembled, sand the entire project and finish it before final assembly. You'll be gluing this bookcase together in one operation, which includes 22 biscuits and a dozen clamps, so gather all the necessary materials before final assembly and have them within reach.

12 | It took less than 5 minutes to apply the glue to all the parts and clamp them all together. You might need an assistant to help hold the back panel in place and lend a hand attaching the clamps.

bentwood ash
CLOCK

This project was a lot of fun to make. It started out as

a clock mounted inside an arching piece of wood,

then it turned into a clock hanging on a

curving lamppost, but as you can see, it

then became something else! I would en-

courage you to explore the possibilities of bending

wood and see what shapes you can create. The type

of biscuits used on this project are small face-frame

biscuits; I found that they made the leg assembly

much stronger than just a plain butt joint.

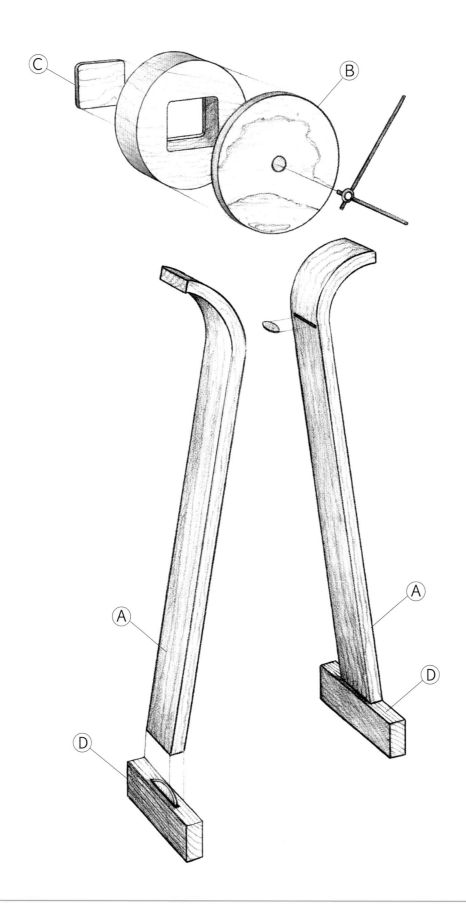

CUTTING LIST (INCHES) • bentwood ash clock

REF.	QTY.	PART	STOCK	THICKNESS	WIDTH	LENGTH	COMMENTS
A	2	Legs	Ash	$^9/_{16}$	2	15	
B	1	Face	Ash	$1^3/_4$	5	5	
C	1	Back Plate	Ash	$^1/_4$	$2^7/_8$	$2^7/_8$	
D	2	Feet	Walnut*	$^5/_8$	$1^1/_4$	$4^1/_4$	*Your choice of wood type
	2	No. 4 x $^5/_8$" Brass Flathead Screws					
	1	Set of Clockworks for $^1/_4$"-Thick Face					

CUTTING LIST (MILLIMETERS) • bentwood ash clock

REF.	QTY.	PART	STOCK	THICKNESS	WIDTH	LENGTH	COMMENTS
A	2	Legs	Ash	14	51	381	
B	1	Face	Ash	45	127	127	
C	1	Back Plate	Ash	6	73	73	
D	2	Feet	Walnut*	16	32	108	*Your choice of wood type
	2	No. 4 x 16mm Brass Flathead Screws					
	1	Set of Clockworks for 6mm-Thick Face					

1 Set the table saw fence at $^3/_{32}$" and rip six strips of wood. Use an orienting triangle to keep the strips in order as they come off the stock piece.

2 If you use a very sharp saw blade and feed the wood through the saw at a steady rate, you will get good, clean cuts on the strips of wood. These strips can be glued as they come off of the saw, or you could smooth them a bit with a hand plane or a thickness sander. After applying glue to all of the strips, bend them around a form (see the sidebar "Making a Bending Form" on page 37 for the technique). You might need an assistant for this operation. Let the glue cure overnight. When I took this lamination off of the form, I expected some springback because this is a fairly tight bend, but it had none.

BENTWOOD ASH CLOCK *continued*

3 Originally, I was going to leave the bent wood as it came off of the form, but creativity got the best of me and I changed my design. For this particular project, I split the lamination in half.

4 I dry clamped the two legs (that's what I decided they would become) as shown in Photo 7 and put a straightedge across the feet. I drew lines to show the angles that the feet would need to have so the clock would stand up. I then set the table saw miter gauge to the angle needed for the feet and set the fence to the height of the legs. This operation can be safely done by keeping the leg tight against the miter gauge fence.

5 This is the setup I used to cut the biscuit slots in the legs at the point where they come together. This cut is made with the small cutter installed in the biscuit joiner for a face-frame biscuit.

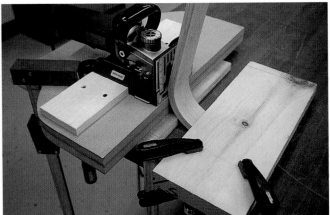

6 Another view of the jig.

7 | This is one of the simplest glue-ups I've ever done!

8 | The face of the clock started out as a solid block of wood. I first cut off the ¼"-thick face. Do this on the table saw by making one-half of the cut, then turn the block over and make the final cut. (You could make this cut using a band saw, but the cut won't be as smooth.) On the remaining block I made two cuts with the grain, making sure that the center cutout (this cutout includes two widths of the saw blade) was the width of the clockworks. I then crosscut the center block twice, making sure the center cutout (again, this cutout includes two widths of the saw blade) was the width of the clockworks, and then removed the center piece. This is the safest way to create the cavity for the clockworks. (If you have round clockworks, you could simply drill a large-diameter hole.)

9 | Keep all the parts in order and glue them together. I was amazed at how well the grain patterns came back together and the block looked like the original solid piece of wood!

10 Draw a circle the size of the clock face onto the blank, and cut just outside of the line with a band saw or jigsaw. I used a stationary sander to smooth the edges of the clock. A belt sander clamped upside down in a bench vise would also do the job.

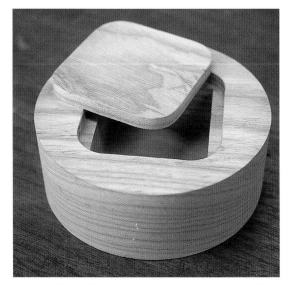

11 Use a rabbet-cutting bit in a router to cut the lip for the lid. Then cut and fit the lid to the cutout.

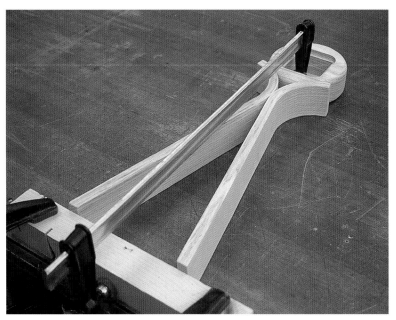

12 Glue the clock face to the legs. I didn't use any biscuits or screws for this operation. Just a small amount of glue will hold it all together. Use a light clamping pressure.

13 | Attach the lid with two small brass screws.

14 | I decided that the clock needed feet, so I cut a small biscuit slot in the bottom of each leg.

15 | After cutting, shaping and slotting the feet, I finished them and then glued them in place. Making these feet (if you decide you need them) is purely a subjective process, and you should use your imagination to create your own special feet!

red oak
MIRROR FRAME

This mirror frame is influenced by a Greene and

Greene mirror frame I once saw in a photograph. I

sized it from the photo and kept the basic

shape. The Greene and Greene style

has rounded cutouts and edges and

uses pine with a warm brown color that

gives the piece a soft look and feel. I used red

oak and made square cutouts in the top rail of

the frame, beveled all the edges of the frame parts

and stained it a medium-brown color.

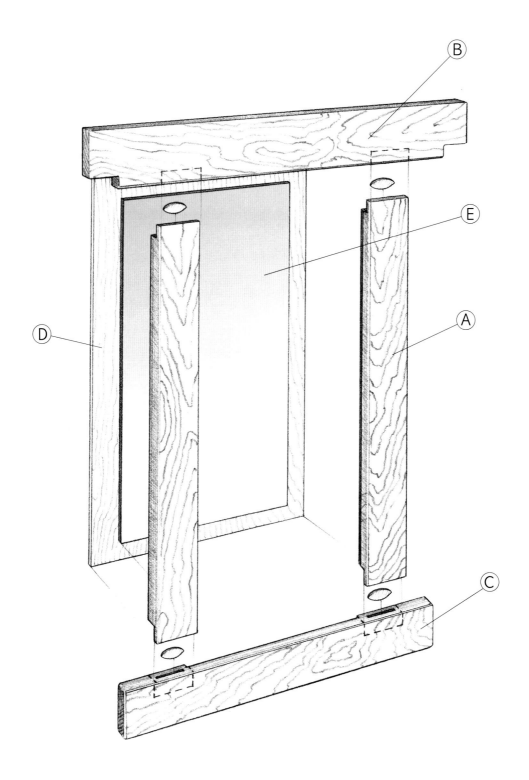

CUTTING LIST (INCHES) • red oak mirror frame

REF.	QTY.	PART	STOCK	THICKNESS	WIDTH	LENGTH	COMMENTS
A	2	Stiles	Red Oak	7/8	4	33³⁄₄	
B	1	Top Rail	Red Oak	5/8	5	40	
C	1	Bottom Rail	Red Oak	5/8	4	32	
D	1	Back	Luan Ply	1/4	24	36	
E	1	Mirror	Glass	1/4	20³⁄₄	33¹⁄₄	
	16	No. 6 x 3/4" Flathead Screws					
	2	Hangers					

CUTTING LIST (MILLIMETERS) • red oak mirror frame

REF.	QTY.	PART	STOCK	THICKNESS	WIDTH	LENGTH	COMMENTS
A	2	Stiles	Red Oak	22	102	857	
B	1	Top Rail	Red Oak	16	127	1016	
C	1	Bottom Rail	Red Oak	16	102	813	
D	1	Back	Luan Ply	6	610	914	
E	1	Mirror	Glass	6	527	844	
	16	No. 6 x 19mm Flathead Screws					
	2	Hangers					

1 Use the table saw to cut the rabbets in the ends of the stile. Make the vertical cut first. Be sure that the saw table and the throat plate are waxed so that the material will feed through the saw smoothly. If you like, use a scrap piece of wood to back up this cutting operation.

2 | Lay the stile down flat and make the second cut to complete the rabbet.

3 | This is the finished rabbet cut.

4 | Cut the notches in the ends of the top frame rail. Use a miter gauge with a fence and make the vertical cut first.

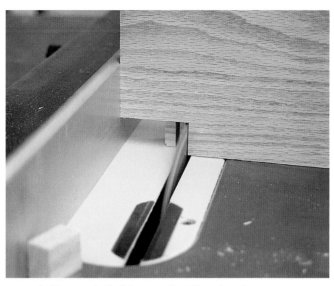

5 | Cut away half of the waste first. Complete the notch with a second cut.

6 | I used the jointer to cut the bevel on the long edges of the frame parts.

7 A block plane works very well for cutting the bevels on the ends of the frame parts.

8 The bevels on the notches at the ends of the top rail can be cut with a file.

9 Lay out the frame and mark the location of the biscuit slots. Rest the base of the biscuit joiner in the rabbet on the stiles, and cut the slots.

10 Turn the top and bottom rails facedown, and cut slots that match up with the slots in the ends of the stiles.

11 | Use four No. 20 biscuits and glue the frame together. Note the spacers to keep the stiles aligned properly.

12 | After the glue has cured, rout a rabbet in the back of the frame. Use a chisel to square the corners of the rabbet.

13 | I routed the rabbet $\frac{1}{32}$" deeper than the thickness of the mirror. When the mirror was installed, I put a cardboard spacer between the mirror and the back panel. This cardboard pads the mirror and protects the silvering on the back of the mirror.

free-form
PLANT STAND

When I began to write this book, this plant stand was the first project I started to build. Several months later, it was the last project I finished. I had a lot of fun fussing with it; it was a constant work in progress during the course of writing the book. Originally, it started out as a lamp. (Shouldn't every book have some sort of lamp?) Somewhere between the designing and the building process, this project turned itself upside down and became a plant stand!

This project shows that the biscuit joiner can be used for practically any kind of construction. I made the three-way joint with four face-frame biscuits and polyurethane glue. Surprisingly, the joint turned out to be very strong.

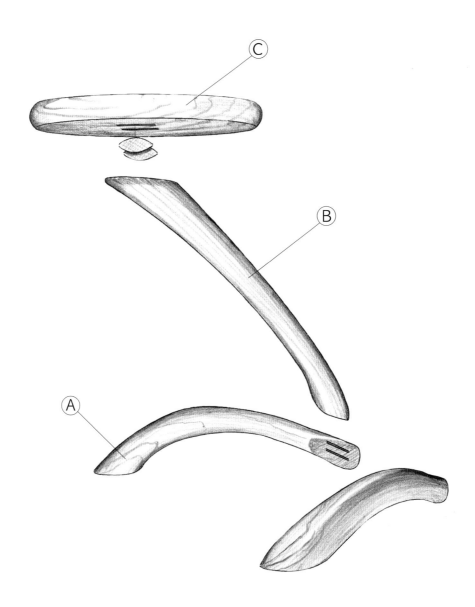

CUTTING LIST (INCHES) free-form plant stand

REF.	QTY.	PART	STOCK	THICKNESS	WIDTH	LENGTH	COMMENTS
A	2	Legs	Walnut	2+/–	3+/–	14+/–	
B	1	Arm	Walnut	2+/–	3+/–	18+/–	
C	1	Top Plate	Ash*	1	8¼ dia.		*Wood of your choice

CUTTING LIST (MILLIMETERS) free-form plant stand

REF.	QTY.	PART	STOCK	THICKNESS	WIDTH	LENGTH	COMMENTS
A	2	Legs	Walnut	51+/–	76+/–	356+/–	
B	1	Arm	Walnut	51+/–	76+/–	457+/–	
C	1	Top Plate	Ash*	25mm	209 dia.		*Wood of your choice

1 I had a chunk of walnut in my wood stash, and it seemed to be the material to use for this project. I sketched the shape of the three parts (legs or arms?) on the wood blank and cut them out on the band saw.

2 Cut flats on the ends of the two legs. I used a table saw, but you could make the cuts on a band saw and sand them flat using a belt sander or a stationary sander. The flats could also be made using a block plane or file.

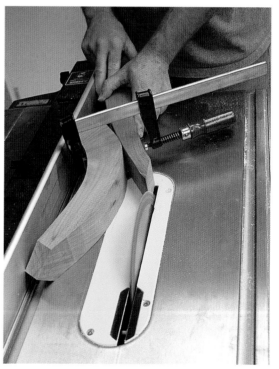

3 Cut the flat on the arm. Again, use whatever tool works best for you.

4 Before gluing the three-way joint, I shaped the legs and arm using a spokeshave.

5 Use two face-frame biscuits stacked together. This is much stronger than using just a single biscuit.

6 Glue the two legs together first, then glue the arm in place. Note the use of tread tape to keep the clamp from slipping. I used polyurethane glue because it holds end-grain joints together very well. Dip the biscuits in water, then apply the glue.

7 To level the plant stand and let the feet sit flat, put the project on a flat surface and scribe the material that needs to be removed. You may have to repeat this step a couple times.

8 The rough shaping is best done with a wood rasp.

9 Start sanding with 80-grit sandpaper and progress to finer and finer grits, ending with 220 grit.

10 The top plate is a scrap piece of ash, but any wood of your choice will work. I lightened the look of the top by beveling both the top and the bottom edge. After the final finish is dry, cut slots for two biscuits in the base and the top. Glue it all together and you're done!

sycamore
CHEST OF DRAWERS

This large dresser is another Shaker piece I sized and detailed

from a photograph. It is a piece that was originally made

around 1840 in Union Village, Ohio. The curved

and scrolled feet are indicative of the Ohio

Shakers, as this would have been a little too fancy

for the Shakers living farther south in Ken-

tucky. The original in the photo

was made of tiger maple and

poplar. I chose to make this proj-

ect out of quartersawn sycamore and soft maple. This project

shows that modern joinery techniques can be easily adapted to

traditional furniture making.

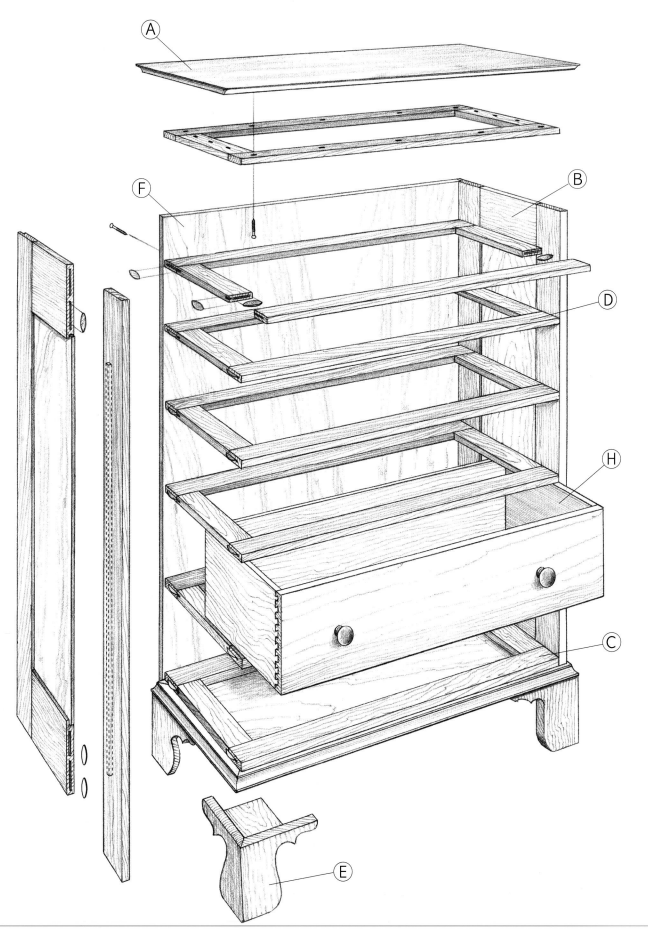

CUTTING LIST (INCHES) • sycamore chest of drawers

REF.	QTY.	PART	MATERIAL	THICKNESS	WIDTH	LENGTH	COMMENTS
A	1	Top	QS Syc*	$7/8$	20	42	*QS Syc = Quartersawn Sycamore
Sides							
B	2	Sides	QS Syc	$13/16$	19	$47\frac{1}{2}$	Finished dimensions of assembled sides
SIDE PARTS	4	Stiles	QS Syc	$13/16$	4	$47\frac{1}{2}$	
	2	Top Rails	QS Syc	$13/16$	$6\frac{1}{2}$	11	
	2	Bottom Rails	QS Syc	$13/16$	7	11	
	2	Panels	QS Syc	$1/4$	12	35	
Bottom Frame							
C	1	Bottom Frame		$13/16$	20	42	Finished dimensions of assembled frame
FRAME PARTS	1	Front Rail	QS Syc	$13/16$	4	42	
	2	Side Rails	QS Syc	$13/16$	4	20	
	1	Back Rail	Soft Maple	$13/16$	4	34	
Web Frames							
D	7	Web Frames		$3/4$	$18\frac{1}{2}$	$38\frac{1}{4}$	Finished dimensions of assembled frame
WEB PARTS	7	Front Rails	QS Syc	$3/4$	3	$38\frac{1}{4}$	
	7	Back Rails	Soft Maple	$3/4$	3	$38\frac{1}{4}$	
	14	Side Rails	Soft Maple	$3/4$	3	$12\frac{1}{2}$	
E	8	Feet	QS Syc	$13/16$	6	6	
F	1	Back	Birch Ply	$1/2$	$39\frac{1}{2}$	$48\frac{3}{8}$	

REF.	QTY.	PART	MATERIAL	H	W	D	COMMENTS
Drawers							
G	2	Drawers		$8\frac{3}{4}$	$38\frac{1}{4}$	$18\frac{3}{8}$	Finished dimensions of assembled drawer
DRAWER PARTS	4	Sides	Soft Maple	$5/8$	$8\frac{3}{4}$	$17\frac{3}{4}$	
	2	Backs	Soft Maple	$5/8$	$8\frac{3}{4}$	$38\frac{1}{4}$	
	2	Fronts	QS Syc	$13/16$	$8\frac{3}{4}$	$38\frac{1}{4}$	
	2	Bottoms	Luan Ply	$1/4$	$17\frac{1}{2}$	$37\frac{5}{8}$	
H	2	Drawers		$7\frac{1}{4}$	$38\frac{1}{4}$	$18\frac{3}{8}$	Finished dimensions of assembled drawer
DRAWER PARTS	2	Sides	Soft Maple	$5/8$	$7\frac{1}{4}$	$17\frac{3}{4}$	
	1	Back	Soft Maple	$5/8$	$7\frac{1}{4}$	$38\frac{1}{4}$	
	1	Front	QS Syc	$13/16$	$7\frac{1}{4}$	$38\frac{1}{4}$	
	1	Bottom	Luan Ply	$1/4$	$17\frac{1}{2}$	$37\frac{5}{8}$	
J	1	Drawer		6	$38\frac{1}{4}$	$18\frac{3}{8}$	Finished dimensions of assembled drawer
DRAWER PARTS	2	Sides	Soft Maple	$5/8$	6	$17\frac{3}{4}$	
	1	Back	Soft Maple	$5/8$	6	$38\frac{1}{4}$	
	1	Front	QS Syc	$13/16$	6	$38\frac{1}{4}$	
	1	Bottom	Luan Ply	$1/4$	$17\frac{1}{2}$	$37\frac{5}{8}$	
K	1	Drawer		$4\frac{1}{4}$	$38\frac{1}{4}$	$18\frac{3}{8}$	Finished dimensions of assembled drawer
DRAWER PARTS	2	Sides	Soft Maple	$5/8$	$4\frac{1}{4}$	$17\frac{3}{4}$	
	1	Back	Soft Maple	$5/8$	$4\frac{1}{4}$	$38\frac{1}{4}$	
	1	Front	QS Syc	$13/16$	$4\frac{1}{4}$	$38\frac{1}{4}$	
	1	Bottom	Luan Ply	$1/4$	$17\frac{1}{2}$	$37\frac{5}{8}$	

CUTTING LIST (MILLIMETERS) • sycamore chest of drawers

REF.	QTY.	PART	MATERIAL	THICKNESS	WIDTH	LENGTH	COMMENTS
A	1	Top	QS Syc*	22	508	1067	*QS Syc = Quartersawn Sycamore

Sides

REF.	QTY.	PART	MATERIAL	THICKNESS	WIDTH	LENGTH	COMMENTS
B	2	Sides	QS Syc	21	483	1207	Finished dimensions of assembled sides
SIDE PARTS	4	Stiles	QS Syc	21	102	1207	
	2	Top Rails	QS Syc	21	165	279	
	2	Bottom Rails	QS Syc	21	178	279	
	2	Panels	QS Syc	6	305	889	

Bottom Frame

REF.	QTY.	PART	MATERIAL	THICKNESS	WIDTH	LENGTH	COMMENTS
C	1	Bottom Frame		21	508	1067	Finished dimensions of assembled frame
FRAME PARTS	1	Front Rail	QS Syc	21	102	1067	
	2	Side Rails	QS Syc	21	102	508	
	1	Back Rail	Soft Maple	21	102	864	

Web Frames

REF.	QTY.	PART	MATERIAL	THICKNESS	WIDTH	LENGTH	COMMENTS
D	7	Web Frames		19	470	971	Finished dimensions of assembled frame
WEB PARTS	7	Front Rails	QS Syc	19	76	971	
	7	Back Rails	Soft Maple	19	76	971	
	14	Side Rails	Soft Maple	19	76	318	

REF.	QTY.	PART	MATERIAL	THICKNESS	WIDTH	LENGTH	COMMENTS
E	8	Feet	QS Syc	21	152	152	
F	1	Back	Birch Ply	13	1004	1229	

Drawers

REF.	QTY.	PART	MATERIAL	H	W	D	COMMENTS
G	2	Drawers		222	971	467	Finished dimensions of assembled drawer
DRAWER PARTS	4	Sides	Soft Maple	16	222	451	
	2	Backs	Soft Maple	16	222	971	
	2	Fronts	QS Syc	21	222	971	
	2	Bottoms	Luan Ply	6	445	956	
H	2	Drawers		184	971	467	Finished dimensions of assembled drawer
DRAWER PARTS	2	Sides	Soft Maple	16	184	451	
	1	Back	Soft Maple	16	184	971	
	1	Front	QS Syc	21	184	971	
	1	Bottom	Luan Ply	6	445	956	
J	1	Drawer		152	971	467	Finished dimensions of assembled drawer
DRAWER PARTS	2	Sides	Soft Maple	16	152	451	
	1	Back	Soft Maple	16	152	971	
	1	Front	QS Syc	21	152	971	
	1	Bottom	Luan Ply	6	445	956	
K	1	Drawer		108	971	467	Finished dimensions of assembled drawer
DRAWER PARTS	2	Sides	Soft Maple	16	108	451	
	1	Back	Soft Maple	16	108	971	
	1	Front	QS Syc	21	108	971	
	1	Bottom	Luan Ply	6	445	956	

1 Use a ¼" straight bit in a router to cut the stopped dadoes for the ¼" panels in the cabinet sides.

2 This is what the joinery looks like for the stiles and rails of the side panels. The dadoes are stopped, leaving plenty of material for the biscuits. This type of joinery takes less time to create than the traditional mortise-and-tenon joinery.

3 Assembly of the side panels: The resawn ¼" solid-wood panels fit into the stopped dadoes, and the biscuits create the corner joinery.

4 These panels are easy to assemble and clamp together. Work on a flat surface and the panels will align themselves with no twisting.

5 | These are the drawer runner panel assembly parts. The slots for the biscuits can be cut in a matter of minutes when all of the parts are laid out in order.

6 | The bottom frame has mitered corners with biscuits inside to add strength and to help keep the parts in alignment with each other. Lay the frame assembly on two clamps running lengthwise with the frame and apply light clamping pressure. Add clamps at both corners running crosswise to the frame and apply light clamping pressure. Alternate applying clamping pressure lengthwise and crosswise until the miters are tight and aligned at the outer corners. When the glue is dry, sand the frame and cut the cove in the ends and front edges using a ¾" roundnose router bit.

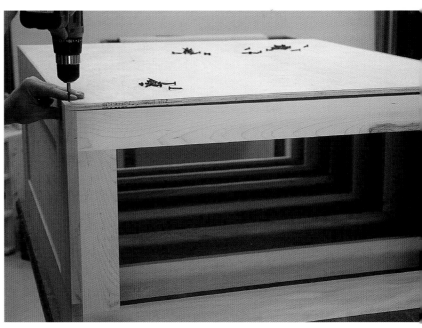

7 | Cut the rabbets in the back edges of the sides using a jointer or a table saw. Then lay the side panels side by side (see Project 2, step 1) and cut the slots for the biscuits for all the drawer runner frames. Cut the slots in the ends of the drawer runner assemblies, gather all the biscuits and clamps you'll need, get an assistant and you're ready to glue up the carcass! Check as you go to make sure the carcass stays square and flat.

8 | The back on the original dresser was made of lap-jointed boards because the Shakers didn't have plywood! I used a piece of ½" plywood for the back and screwed it into place in the rabbets on the sides and the drawer runner panel back rails.

9 | Start with a dimensioned board long enough to cut three or four foot-blocks. Cut the miter on one long edge. Then cut the foot blanks to size. Make a pattern for the foot scroll out of ¼" plywood or stiff cardboard. Trace the outline on all the foot blanks. Be sure to make four left and four right blanks.

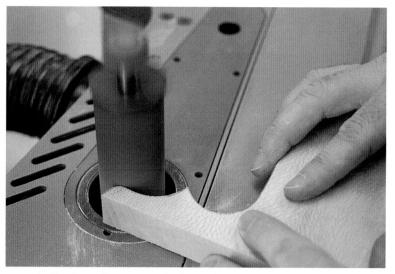

10 | Cut the scroll pattern on the feet as close to the pattern line as possible. Sand up to the line using an orbital sander, a sanding cylinder mounted in a drill press, or a rasp.

11 | Use clear 2"-wide packaging tape to hinge two foot-blocks together.

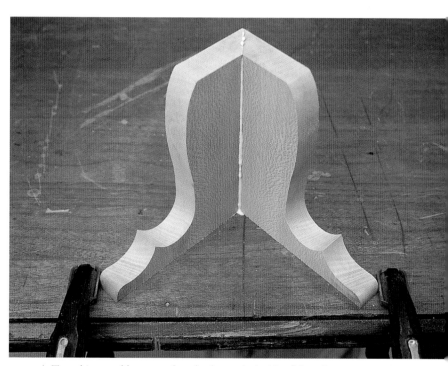

12 | Turn this assembly over and apply glue to the inside of the miter joint. Fold it together and hold it square until the glue sets.

13 Glue a mounting block to each foot assembly.

14 Sand the feet and then attach them to the underside of the bottom frame assembly with glue and screws.

15 Hold each foot back from the front edge of the bottom frame about ⅛". This gives the feet a light, floating look. (I hadn't sanded the feet at this point yet. It is easier to sand the feet first before attaching them to the bottom!)

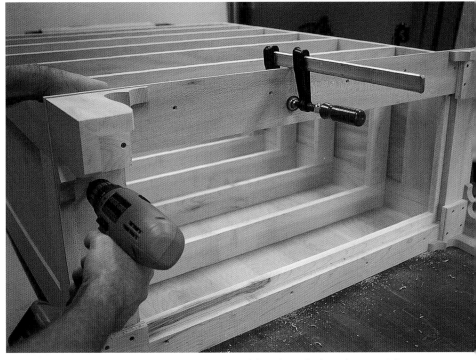

16 Attach the bottom assembly to the bottom of the cabinet body with screws. The top panel is attached to the top of the dresser with screws inserted into oversize holes drilled into the top rail assembly.

17 | I thought that since I was using modern joinery to assemble the dresser body, I should use a modern technique for cutting the dovetails for the drawers. These are called fitted drawers because they are fitted to the opening in the dresser. There is no hardware involved. Set up the template and router per the instructions that come with the dovetail router template. Make test cuts until the setup is right. Take your time and make sure that the dovetails fit snugly. Once you have the setup, you can cut dovetails all day long, and they will be perfect!

18 | A detail shot of the pins for the dovetails. When cutting the dado for the bottom panel, be sure that it is centered in a pin.

19 | Before assembling the drawers, fit the sides of the drawers into each section of the dresser. If any material needs to be removed, cut it from the bottom of the sides. Cut off the same amount of material from the bottom of the drawer front. Then assemble the drawers.

20 | Use a belt sander or bench plane to fit the drawers. After the drawers are finished, apply some paste wax to the drawer runners in the cabinet and to the bottoms of the drawer sides.

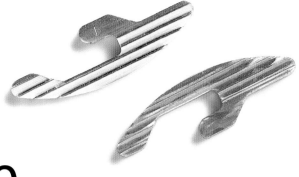

ash armoire
MEDIA CENTER

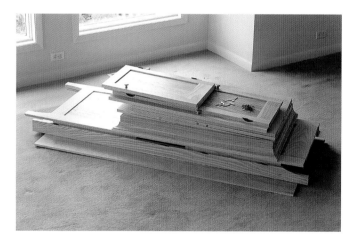

One of the great features of this project is that it can be knocked down into smaller parts. Add a hanging rail in the top section and this cabinet can be used as an armoire. It has as much space as a small closet. It can also be used as a media center, complete with a shelf large enough to hold two or three video components. The drawers can be fitted with CD, DVD or VCR-tape organizers. The back has a removable panel for easy access to all of the electronic components. The panels in the doors and sides are resawn and book-matched. I picked wood with lots of colors and figured grain patterns for these panels and used the straighter-grained pieces for the rails, stiles and legs. The finish is clear lacquer.

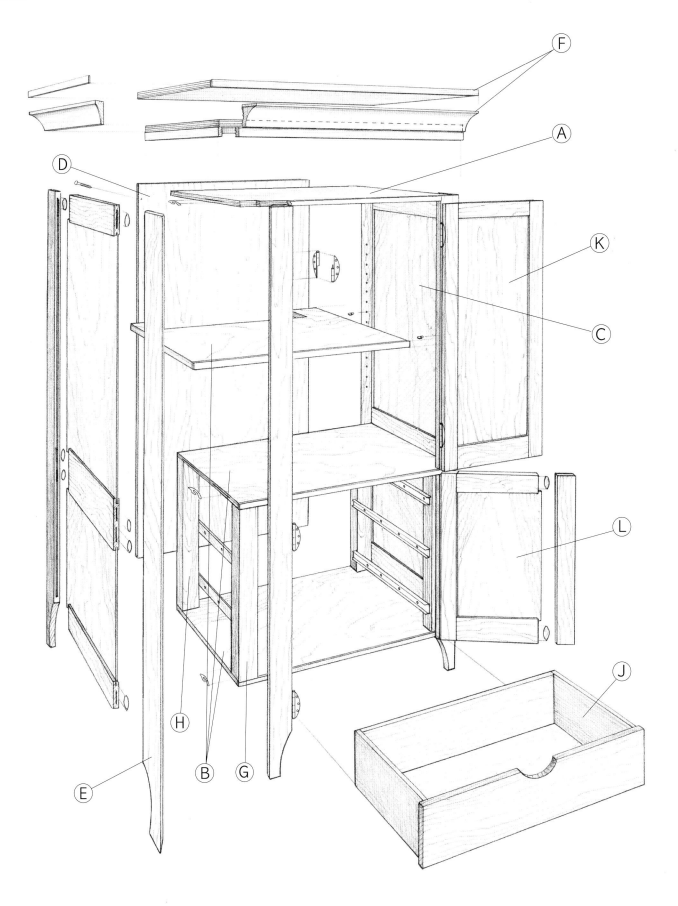

CUTTING LIST (INCHES) • ash armoire/media center

REF.	QTY.	PART	MATERIAL	THICKNESS	WIDTH	LENGTH	COMMENTS
A	1	Top Shelf	Birch Ply	3/4	23 1/2	34 1/2	Includes 1/4" x 3/4" ash strip on shelf front
B	3	Shelves	Birch Ply	3/4	22 3/4	34 1/2	Includes 1/4" x 3/4" ash strip on shelf front
Sides							
C	2	Sides	Ash	3	24	71	Finished dimensions of assembled side
SIDE PARTS (FOR ONE SIDE)	3	Legs	Ash	13/16	3	71	
	1	Top Rail	Ash	13/16	3 3/4	18	
	1	Center Rail	Ash	13/16	5 3/4	18	
	1	Bottom Rail	Ash	13/16	3 1/2	18	
	2	Top Panels	Ash	1/4	19	34 1/4	
	2	Bottom Panels	Ash	1/4	19	19 1/2	
D	1	Back	Birch Ply	1/2	35 1/2	64 3/4	
E	8	Feet	Ash	13/16	6	6	
Top Moulding Assembly							
F	1	Top Moulding Assem.		3 3/4	26 1/2	41	Finished dimensions of assembled top
TOP MOULDING ASSEMBLY PARTS	1	Inner Top Panel	Birch Ply	3/4	24 11/16	37 3/8	
	1	Front Straight Trim	Ash	3/4	1 1/2	37 1/2	
	2	Side Straight Trim	Ash	3/4	1 1/2	24 3/4	
	1	Front Cove Trim	Ash	1 1/2	1 1/2	40 1/2	
	1	Side Cove Trim	Ash	1 1/2	1 1/2	26 1/4	
	1	Outer Top Panel	Birch Ply	3/4	26 1/2	41	Includes 3/8" ash strips on front & sides
	1	Rear Spacer	Birch Ply	3/4	1 1/2	37 3/8	
G	2	Front Drawer Spacers	Ash	2	3 1/2	23	
H	2	Rear Drawer Spacers	Soft Maple	1 1/2	3 1/2	23	
Drawers				**H**	**W**	**D**	
J	3	Drawers		7 1/2	21	26 1/2	Final drawer size (drawer fronts: 27 3/8")
DRRAWER PARTS	6	Sides	Soft Maple	1/2	7 1/2	20	
	3	Backs	Soft Maple	1/2	6 1/4	25 1/2	
	3	Fronts	Ash	3/4	7 1/2	27 3/8	
	3	Bottoms	Luan Ply	1/4	20 1/4	26	
Doors							
K	2	Upper Doors	Ash	13/16	14 7/8	39 1/4	
DOOR PARTS	4	Stiles	Ash	13/16	2 1/4	39 1/4	
	4	Rails	Ash	13/16	2 1/4	10 3/8	
	2	Panels	Ash	1/4	11 3/8	35 3/4	
L	2	Lower Doors	Ash	13/16	14 7/8	24 1/8	
DOOR PARTS	4	Stiles	Ash	13/16	2 1/4	24 1/8	
	4	Rails	Ash	13/16	2 1/4	10 3/8	
	2	Panels	Ash	1/4	11 3/8	20 5/8	

	18	Knockdown Hardware Inserts
	4 pairs	Duplex Hinges
	3 sets	20" Full-Extension Drawer Slides
	4	1" Wooden Pulls
		Two-Part Epoxy

REF.	QTY.	PART	MATERIAL	THICKNESS	WIDTH	LENGTH	COMMENTS
A	1	Top Shelf	Birch Ply	19	597	877	Includes 6 x 19 ash strip on shelf front
B	3	Shelves	Birch Ply	19	578	877	Includes 6 x 19 ash strip on shelf front

Sides

REF.	QTY.	PART	MATERIAL	THICKNESS	WIDTH	LENGTH	COMMENTS
C	2	Sides	Ash	76	610	1803	Finished dimensions of assembled side
SIDE PARTS (FOR ONE SIDE)	3	Legs	Ash	21	76	1803	
		Top Rail	Ash	21	95	457	
	1	Center Rail	Ash	21	146	457	
	1	Bottom Rail	Ash	21	89	457	
	2	Top Panels	Ash	6	483	870	
	2	Bottom Panels	Ash	6	483	509	
D	1	Back	Birch Ply	13	702	1645	
E	8	Feet	QS Syc*	21	152	152	

Top Moulding Assembly

REF.	QTY.	PART	MATERIAL	THICKNESS	WIDTH	LENGTH	COMMENTS
F	1	Top Moulding Assem.		95	673	1041	Finished dimensions of assembled top
TOP MOULDING ASSEMBLY PARTS	1	Inner Top Panel	Birch Ply	19	628	950	
	1	Front Straight Trim	Ash	19	38	953	
	2	Side Straight Trim	Ash	19	38	629	
	1	Front Cove Trim	Ash	38	38	1029	
	1	Side Cove Trim	Ash	38	38	666	
	1	Outer Top Panel	Birch Ply	19	673	1041	Includes 10mm ash strips on front & sides
	1	Rear Spacer	Birch Ply	19	38	950	
G	2	Front Drawer Spacers	Ash	51	89	584	
H	2	Rear Drawer Spacers	Soft Maple	38	89	584	

Drawers

REF.	QTY.	PART	MATERIAL	H	W	D	COMMENTS
J	3	Drawers		191	533	673	Final drawer size (drawer fronts: 696mm)
DRAWER PARTS	6	Sides	Soft Maple	13	191	508	
	3	Backs	Soft Maple	13	158	648	
	3	Fronts	Ash	19	191	696	
	3	Bottoms	Luan Ply	6	514	660	

Doors

REF.	QTY.	PART	MATERIAL	THICKNESS	WIDTH	LENGTH	COMMENTS
K	2	Upper Doors	Ash	21	378	997	
DOOR PARTS	4	Stiles	Ash	21	57	997	
	4	Rails	Ash	21	57	264	
	2	Panels	Ash	6	289	908	
L	2	Lower Doors	Ash	21	378	613	
DOOR PARTS	4	Stiles	Ash	21	57	613	
	4	Rails	Ash	21	57	264	
	2	Panels	Ash	6	289	524	

	18	Knockdown Hardware Inserts					
	4 pairs	Duplex Hinges					
	3 sets	500mm Full-Extension Drawer Slides					
	4	25mm Wooden Pulls					
		Two-Part Epoxy					

1 | Make a template of the curve at the feet, and use it to trace the pattern onto the feet. Rough-cut the waste material away using a jigsaw.

2 | Use the template as a guide and rout the curves smooth.

3 | Cut the miters on the two front-leg assemblies, tape the joint (see Project 9, steps 12-13), and apply glue.

4 | Fold the leg assembly. Use hand screws to hold the assembly square while the glue sets.

5 | Here is another method that works well for holding the assembly square.

6 | Cut the stopped dadoes for the resawn panels in the legs using a ¼" straight router bit. Cut the biscuit slots for the leg and rail joints (see Project 4, steps 3–5). Sand the ¼" panels before assembling the sides. As always, get all the clamps, glue, biscuits and an assistant (if you need one) together before you start assembling.

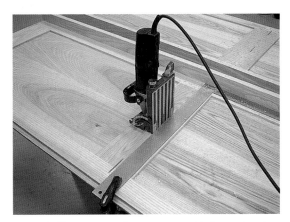

7 | Use a carpenter's square as a guide for cutting the slots for the knockdown hardware. Then cut the slots in the ends of the bottom, the middle and the top shelves for the matching knockdown hardware.

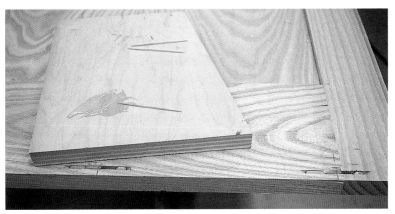

8 | You will need to use a two-part epoxy for gluing the aluminum hardware into the No. 20-sized slots. I mixed a batch of epoxy about the size of a 50-cent piece (remember those?), which was enough to glue up five or six pieces of hardware into the slots. I used toothpicks to put the epoxy into the bottom and halfway up the sides of the slots. Don't use too much epoxy or it will get into the inside of the hook on the knockdown hardware and on the top sides of the slot. This makes it impossible to put the two parts together after the epoxy has cured. I recommend practicing putting the epoxy into the slots in scrap material before starting on the project.

9 Make the top frame. (You could also use a solid piece of plywood.) Then glue the straight part of the top moulding onto the frame, letting the moulding hang over the frame about 1/16". This lip will make it easier to align the cove part of the moulding.

10 I made the cove moulding on the table saw. This has become a common operation, and it is safe if you do it correctly. It works best if you use a sharp, carbide-tooth blade. Before you set up for the cove making, cut a flat face on the moulding material as shown on the piece in the left of the photo above. Set up a fence behind the blade at about a 45° angle to the blade. Clamp it in place and raise the saw blade about 1/8". Test the cut until it is centered in the moulding material and the cove is the proper radius. (To center the cut, move the fence toward or away from the blade, keeping the angle the same. To change the radius, change the angle of the fence.) Make your first cut in all the moulding pieces. Raise the blade another 1/8" (or a little less if your saw sounds like it's working too hard). Continue until the cove depth is to your liking. You will probably need to move the fence slightly toward or away from the blade to keep the cut centered, but try not to change the angle of the fence.

11 Attach the cove moulding to the top frame by holding it against the lip you created with the straight moulding. You can use small brads or nails to attach the moulding. I chose to clamp it in place to avoid nail holes. Then glue the outer top panel to the top of the top moulding assembly.

12 Make the long cut for the notches in the top shelf of the cabinet. These notches will clear the front leg stiles and let the front edge of the shelf come flush to the front legs.

13 | Make the short cut in two passes.

14 | The drawers are made of soft maple with ash fronts. Use a paint can to draw the curve for the hand cutout on the drawer fronts. Make the cutout with a jigsaw and sand smooth.

15 | These drawers use full-extension hardware, so the fronts need to have a ⁷/₁₆" lip extending past both sides. This lip will conceal the hardware when the drawer is closed. The back of the drawer is captured between the sides. Note the spacer to help keep the assembly square.

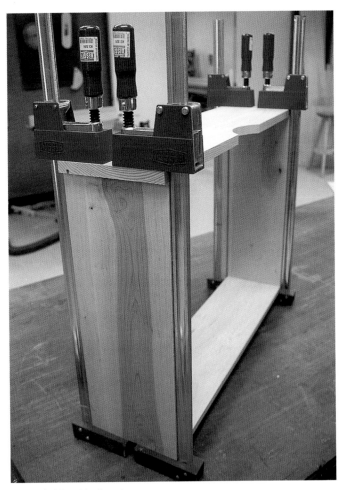

16 | The sides butt into the front.

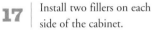

17 Install two fillers on each side of the cabinet.

18 Lay out where the hardware will be mounted on the drawers and transfer this to the cabinet sides. Use spacers to hold the hardware parallel to the cabinet bottom. The spacers also ensure the hardware will be located at the same height on both sides of the cabinet.

20 I used a ¼" wing cutter in the router to cut the stopped dadoes for the door panel. (A ¼" straight bit will work as well.)

19 Making the drawer fronts out of ash gives the cabinet a more formal furniture look. The hardware on the drawers will last for years of openings and closings!

21 This is what the door frame joints look like before assembly. It is a quick and simple way to make frames (with or without panels).

22 The hinges for this cabinet are duplex and can be mortised with the biscuit joiner. For this project, I added an auxiliary fence to the biscuit joiner because the cabinet face is 3" wide and the fence on the tool wouldn't extend that far. Fit the doors with the spacings you want and set the biscuit joiner to cut a No. 20 slot. Center the cutter on the door and cabinet spacing. Then cut the mortise. You will have a mortise cut into both the door and the cabinet side at the same time. (If you prefer, set the cutter to make the entire mortise in the door.)

23 Detail of the mortise and hinge.

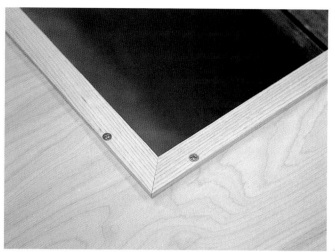

25 Cut out an opening in the upper part of the back panel for cable and wire access. Put a frame around the inside edges of the opening to create a ½" lip.

24 The adjustable shelf needs clearance at the back edge for cables and wires. This is an easy way to create that space. Rip 2" off the back side of the adjustable shelf, then glue two wings to the back of the shelf at both ends. (Use biscuits to hold these wings in place, of course!)

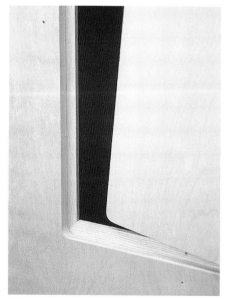

26 Cut a panel to fit in the cutout from the back of the cabinet, and attach it with screws.

27 Use small magnetic catches to hold the doors closed. These are mounted so that both the top and bottom doors use the same magnet; the top door overlays the top half of each magnet, while the bottom door overlays the bottom half of each magnet.

tapered
DRESSER

This design was inspired by photos of straight-line contemporary furniture. It became a fun project because I realized that making these angled joints would be easy. In fact, making these joints using any other method would be tricky, time consuming and in some cases, impossible. When I was in the design-sketching stage, the dresser looked like it needed something to make it complete. The idea of having a jewelery box was appealing. It became a removable box that could be moved to another location if needed. The project has an Art Deco feel and look, so I decided to go one step farther and color the dresser a strong burgundy. The drawer fronts are a medium-brown color, and the whole unit has a clear topcoat of satin precatalyzed lacquer.

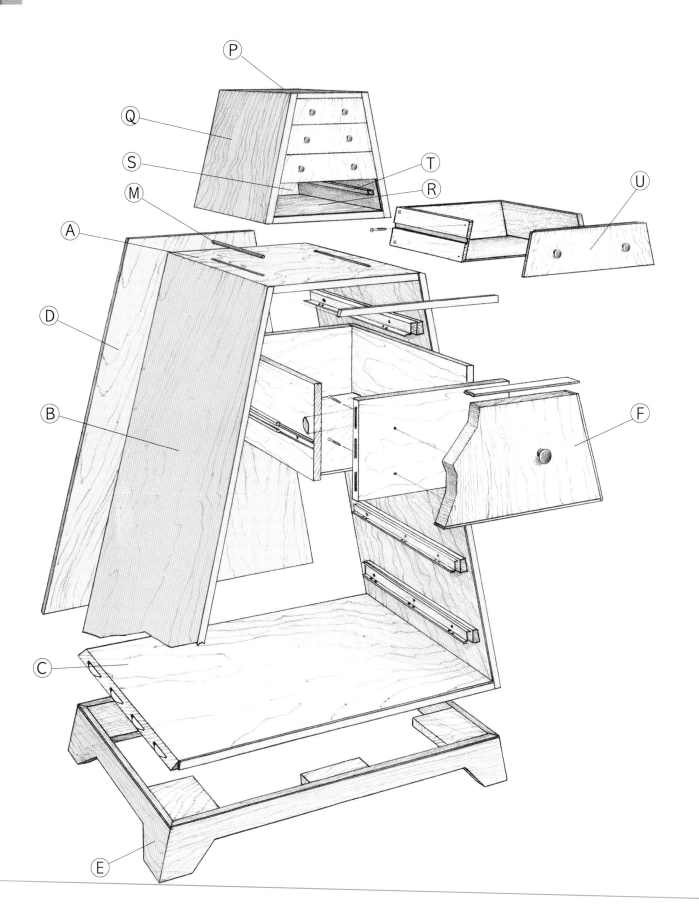

CUTTING LIST (INCHES) • tapered dresser

REF.	QTY.	PART	MATERIAL	THICKNESS	WIDTH	LENGTH	COMMENTS
Base Cabinet							
A	1	Top	Maple Ply	3/4	21 1/2	18 +/-	
B	2	Sides	Maple Ply	3/4	21 1/2	38 1/4 +/-	
C	1	Bottom	Maple Ply	3/4	21 1/2	32 3/4 +/-	
D	1	Back	Birch Ply	1/2	18 – 33	36 (height)	
Base							
E		Base Assembly	Maple	4	22	36	Final size of assembled base
	2	Front & Back Rails	Maple	3/4	4	36	
	2	Side Rails	Maple	3/4	4 1/4 *	22	*Extra width is for cutting angles on edges
	4	Corner Gussets	Maple Ply	3/4	4	4	
	4	Cleats	Maple Ply	3/4	2	4	
F	10	Drawer Mounting Cleats	Maple	3/4	2	19 3/4	
Drawers							
G	1	Drawer Front #1	Maple Ply	3/4	6	19 1/2 +/-	
	2	Sides	Maple	1/2	5 1/2	20	
	2	Front & Back	Maple	1/2	5 1/2	15 1/2	
	1	Bottom	Luan Ply	1/4	16	19 1/2	
H	1	Drawer Front #2	Maple Ply	3/4	6	22 1/2 +/-	
	2	Sides	Maple	1/2	6 1/2	20	
	2	Front & Back	Maple	1/2	6 1/2	18	
	1	Bottom	Luan Ply	1/4	18 1/2	19 1/2	
J	1	Drawer Front #3	Maple Ply	3/4	6	25 1/2 +/-	
	2	Sides	Maple	1/2	6 1/2	20	
	2	Front & Back	Maple	1/2	6 1/2	21	
	1	Bottom	Luan Ply	1/4	21 1/2	19 1/2	
K	1	Drawer Front #4	Maple Ply	3/4	6	28 1/2 +/-	
	2	Sides	Maple	1/2	6 1/2	20	
	2	Front & Back	Maple	1/2	6 1/2	24 1/8	
	1	Bottom	Luan Ply	1/4	24 5/8	19 1/2	
L	1	Drawer Front #5	Maple Ply	3/4	6	32 1/2 +/-	
	2	Sides	Maple	1/2	8 1/4	20	
	2	Front & Back	Maple	1/2	8 1/4	28	
	1	Bottom	Luan Ply	1/4	28 1/2	19 1/2	
M	2	Locating Dowels	Birch	1/2 dia.		10	
		Material for Back Cleats	Maple	1/2	1/2	11 feet	
		Material for Edging	Maple	1/4	13/16	45 feet	
	5 sets	20" Drawer Slides					
	10	Drawer Pulls					
Jewelry Box Case							
P	1	Top	Maple Ply	3/4	11 1/2	10 +/-	
Q	2	Sides	Maple Ply	3/4	11 1/2	10 3/4 +/-	
R	1	Bottom	Maple Ply	3/4	11 1/2	13 7/8 +/-	
S	1	Back	Birch Ply	1/2	9 – 13 1/2	9 (height)	
T	10	Drawer Runners	Maple	1/2	1/2	10 3/8	See text for cutting the angles on two edges
U	1	Drawer Front Material	Maple Ply	3/4	9 – 13 1/2	10 +/- (height)	See drawing for heights of drawer fronts
		Drawer Sides & Backs	Maple	1/2	2 – 2 1/2	12 feet	See drawing for drawer construction details
	8	Drawer Pulls					

CUTTING LIST (MILLIMETERS) • tapered dresser

REF.	QTY.	PART	MATERIAL	THICKNESS	WIDTH	LENGTH	COMMENTS
Base Cabinet							
A	1	Top	Maple Ply	19	546	457$^{+/-}$	
B	2	Sides	Maple Ply	19	546	971$^{+/-}$	
C	1	Bottom	Maple Ply	19	546	832$^{+/-}$	
D	1	Back	Birch Ply	13	457-838	914 (height)	
Base							
E		Base Assembly	Maple	102	559	914	Final size of assembled base
	2	Front & Back Rails	Maple	19	102	914	
BASE PARTS	2	Side Rails	Maple	19	108*	559	*Extra width is for cutting angles on edges
	4	Corner Gussets	Maple Ply	19	102	102	
	4	Cleats	Maple Ply	19	51	102	
F	10	Drawer Mounting Cleats	Maple	19	51	502	
Drawers							
G	1	Drawer Front #1	Maple Ply	19	152	496$^{+/-}$	
	2	Sides	Maple	13	140	508	
	2	Front & Back	Maple	13	140	394	
	1	Bottom	Luan Ply	6	406	496	
H	1	Drawer Front #2	Maple Ply	19	152	572$^{+/-}$	
	2	Sides	Maple	13	165	508	
	2	Front & Back	Maple	13	165	457	
	1	Bottom	Luan Ply	6	470	496	
J	1	Drawer Front #3	Maple Ply	19	152	648$^{+/-}$	
	2	Sides	Maple	13	165	508	
	2	Front & Back	Maple	13	165	533	
	1	Bottom	Luan Ply	6	546	496	
K	1	Drawer Front #4	Maple Ply	19	152	724$^{+/-}$	
	2	Sides	Maple	13	165	508	
	2	Front & Back	Maple	13	165	613	
	1	Bottom	Luan Ply	6	626	496	
L	1	Drawer Front #5	Maple Ply	19	152	826$^{+/-}$	
	2	Sides	Maple	13	209	508	
	2	Front & Back	Maple	13	209	711	
	1	Bottom	Luan Ply	6	724	496	
M	2	Locating Dowels	Birch	13 dia.		254	
		Material for Back Cleats	Maple	13	13	3355	
		Material for Edging	Maple	6	21	13725	
	5 sets	500mm Drawer Slides					
	10	Drawer Pulls					
Jewelry Box Case							
P	1	Top	Maple Ply	19	292	254$^{+/-}$	
Q	2	Sides	Maple Ply	19	292	273$^{+/-}$	
R	1	Bottom	Maple Ply	19	292	352$^{+/-}$	
S	1	Back	Birch Ply	13	229-343	229 (height)	
T	10	Drawer Runners	Maple	13	13	264	See text for cutting the angles on two edges
U	1	Drawer Front Material	Maple Ply	19	229-343	254$^{+/-}$ (height)	See drawing for heights of drawer fronts
		Drawer Sides & Backs	Maple	13	51-64	3660	See drawing for drawer construction details
	8	Drawer Pulls					

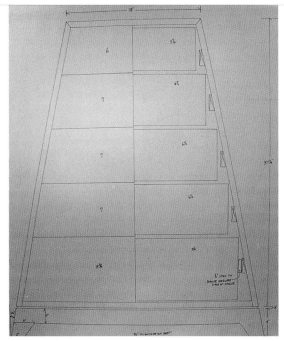

1 To get a clear picture of this dresser, draw a full-scale working drawing. You will be referring to this drawing throughout the making of the dresser.

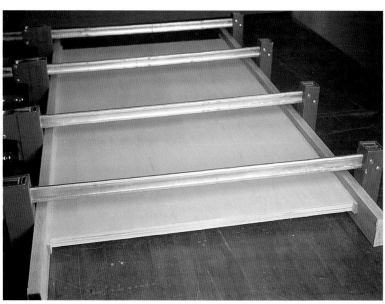

2 Cut the cabinet sides, bottom and top panels to ½" less than the finished width. Leave them about 2" longer than the finished length. Then glue ¼"-thick, solid-wood maple strips on the front and back edges of these cabinet parts.

3 Trim the wood edging flush to the surface of the panels. Using a block plane is the easiest method. Leave the edge slightly proud of the surface of the panel, and sand the edging flush to the panel's surface with a flat sanding block.

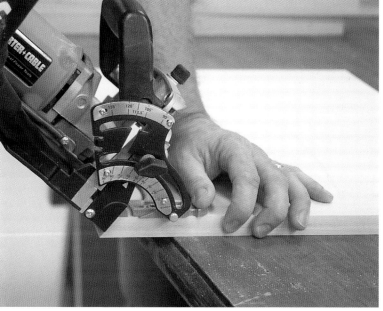

4 Use the table saw to cut the sides, top and bottom panels to their finished lengths with miters. Dry fit the panels by standing them on edge on the full-scale drawing. Adjust the miter angles if needed. This may take two or three times to get it all to fit together. Set the biscuit joiner to the angle of the top miter and use the No. 20 slot setting. Set the cutter so it will cut the slot about ⅛" from the inside of the miter. Double-check your setup on a scrap cut with the same miter angle. Cut the slots in the top panel miters and the top miters in the side panels using this setup.

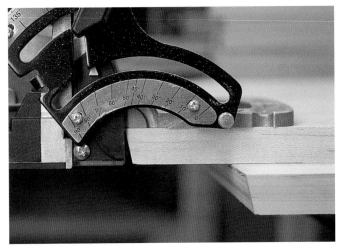

5 | Set the biscuit joiner to 90° and cut the slots at the bottom of the side panels. Note that you're referencing the biscuit joiner from the bottom and inside of the side panels. (I found it helpful to draw on the full-scale drawing where the biscuits would be located in the joints. This helped me to see very clearly where I needed to cut the slots, i.e., in the end of a panel or on the flat of a panel.)

6 | Remember that you need to reference this cut from the bottom of the bottom panel. Make a test cut in a scrap, insert a biscuit and fit this test piece to the bottom of the side panel. Make sure the bottom of the test piece and the bottom of the side panel are flush. If not, make the adjustment to the biscuit joiner and test again. When it's right, cut the slots in the ends of the bottom panel.

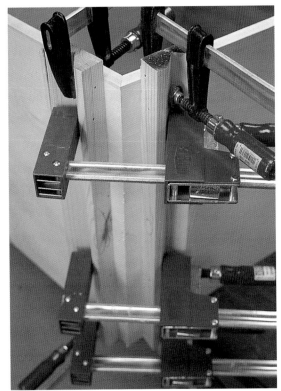

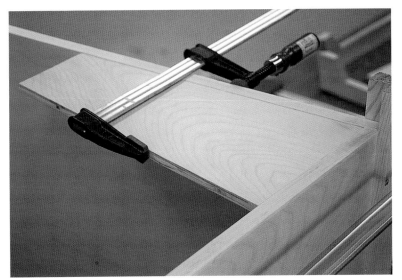

8 | Cut two plywood templates to hold the cabinet in proper alignment.

7 | This is the setup I used to assemble the miter joints. Cut a V-groove in the gluing cauls. Clamp these cauls to the panels, then glue and clamp across the miter as shown. I would recommend using an assistant for this assembly. Glue all four miter joints at the same time so that the cabinet body can be aligned properly.

9 First cut the 13° angles on the top and bottom edges of the side foot rails.

10 Set the miter gauge to a 77° angle and tilt the saw blade to 45°. Cut the front and rear foot rails to length. Then set the miter gauge to 90°, leave the saw blade at 45°, and cut the side foot rails to length. Remember to mark the right and left ends on all the rails.

11 To make the cutouts in the foot rails, transfer the angle from the full-scale drawings to the foot rails. Make the angled cut first. The top of the foot is 3" from the end of the foot rail; the bottom of the foot is 2" from the end.

12 Cut off the top part of the foot rails. This will separate the feet from the rail.

TAPERED DRESSER *continued*

13 | Remove the center off-fall piece, leaving just the feet.

14 | Glue the feet onto the rails.

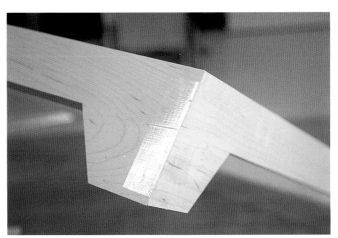

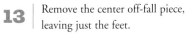

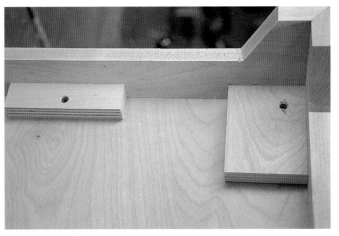

15 | All four pieces can be glued together at the same time. (Use clear packaging tape to hinge the foot rail miters.) Spread out the foot rails miter to miter and tape three joint hinges. Have an assistant help you turn this assembly over, apply glue to the miters and fold it up. Apply glue on the last open miter and tape it together. Voila! Instant base! One more thing you will want to do is cut a ¼" × ¼" rabbet in the top edge of all four base foot rails using the table saw. After the base was glued together, I cut the rabbets using the jointer. If you don't have a jointer, cut the rabbets on the table saw before assembling the base.

16 | Glue ¾" plywood gussets at all four corners of the base and one each on the long sides in the middle. Attach the base with screws to the bottom of the cabinet.

17 | Install the ½" × ½" cleats on the inside of the cabinet with brads or pins, setting the cleats in from the back edge ½".

18 | Fit the back panel to the back of the cabinet as tightly as you can. Using a washer with a ⅛"-thick ring, trace around the inside edge of the cabinet onto the back panel. Remove the panel and trim it to the lines you just drew. (As an alternative, you can cut a ⅛" × ⅛" rabbet around the edges of the back panel.)

19 | Use ⅛" spacers to hold the back panel in place while you attach the panel with glue and screws from the inside of the cabinet.

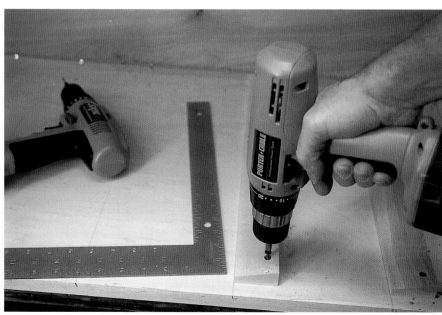

20 | The drawer slide hardware mounting strips have the same angle as the bottom-to-the-side. Locate these strips according to the measurements on the full-scale drawing.

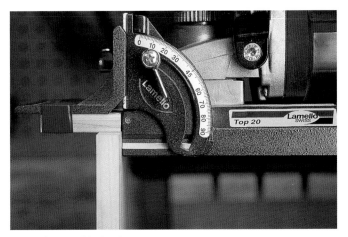

21 | Attach the hardware to the mounting strips, using a scrap of wood to register the hardware in line with the strips.

22 | Assemble the drawer boxes with biscuits.

23 | Because these drawers will have separate fronts, the boxes are fast and easy to assemble.

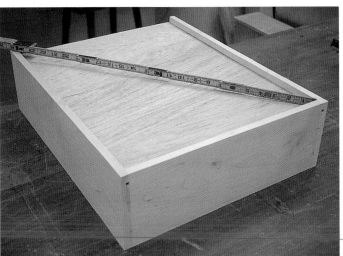

24 | When installing the drawer bottom panels, be sure the drawer box is square (the two diagonals should be equal in length) before inserting the screws through the bottom panel and into the bottom of the box back panel.

25 Attach the hardware to the drawer boxes and install the drawers. If needed, adjust the hardware on the drawers, so the drawer's top, outside edges will not scrape the cabinet.

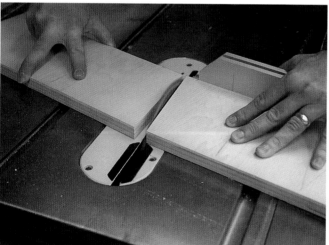

26 The cabinet plywood is bookmatched veneer, so I put the veneer seam in the center of the fronts and cut all the fronts out of the same piece of plywood. First, crosscut the drawers to ¼" less than the finished heights. Next, cut the fronts to width at the angle of the sides to the bottom as shown in the photo. Have the cabinet sitting on a flat and level surface. Check the width of the drawer fronts as you're cutting them. You want to have a ¼" gap around all the edges of the drawer fronts when you are finished cutting them out.

27 Glue ¼"-thick strips of maple on the side edges of the drawer fronts. This method uses the scrap off-fall from cutting out the drawer fronts. To hold the strips in place, clamp two scraps to a flat worktop and simply wedge the drawer front between them.

TAPERED DRESSER *continued*

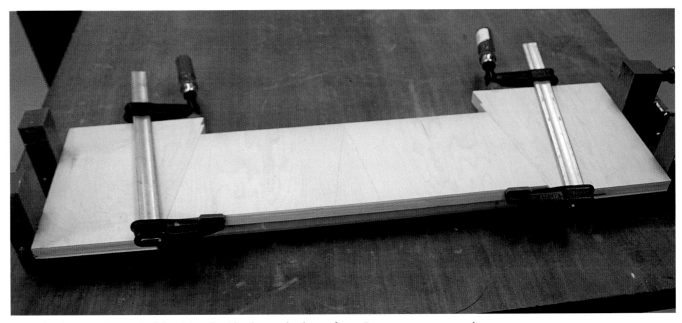

28 This is another method for gluing the side edges to the drawer fronts. Lay two scraps on two clamps, wedge the drawer front and strips between them and clamp it all up. This method allows much more clamping pressure to be used, so be careful not to overtighten the clamps.

29 Trim the side edge strips flush to the top and bottom edges of the drawer fronts.

30 Glue the strips on the top edges of the drawer fronts. Trim these flush with the side edges after the glue sets.

31 This is the final fitting of the drawer fronts. Because there is ¼" of hardwood on three edges of each front, you have the flexibility of trimming away some of this material if needed. Work your way up from the bottom.

32 Take your time fitting the fronts. The spaces around the fronts are critical to the overall look of this piece, and your eye will pick up any discrepancies.

33 Detail of fitted drawer fronts.

34 I used drawer-front adjusters (available from Woodworker's Hardware) to mount the fronts onto the drawer boxes. The machine screw can be tightened and it will hold the front in place. When the drawer is put into the cabinet and any adjustment is needed, the front can be moved up to $^{3}/_{32}$" in any direction. When all is aligned and the dresser has been finished, permanent screws can be installed to hold the drawer front in place.

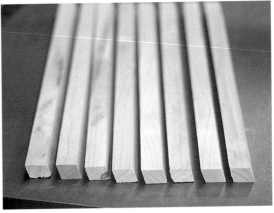

35 The jewelery box is constructed the same way as the dresser. Because the box is small, no drawer hardware is available. The drawers will glide on side runners.

36 After the jewelry cabinet has been assembled, the side runners can be installed using brads or pin nails. To keep the runners square with the front edges of the cabinet, and to hold them parallel to each other, use spacers as shown here. The spacers also ensure that the runners will be the same height on both sides of the cabinet.

37 Cut the drawer sides as shown in the drawing. The rabbet for the drawer bottom panel can be cut on the table saw or on the jointer as shown here. The drawer fronts have rabbets in each end to accept the drawer sides. I assembled these drawers with screws. Biscuits could be used, but you would need to notch the biscuits for the dadoes in the drawer sides.

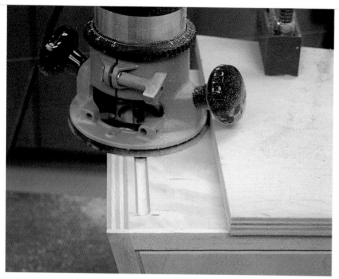

38 The jewelry box is removable from the dresser, but to hold it in place when it's on the dresser, rout two half-round grooves into the top of the dresser. Rout two matching grooves into the bottom of the jewelry box. Cut the groove using a roundnose bit with a ¼" radius. Cut two ½" hardwood dowels to fit into the grooves in the top of the dresser. Apply a little glue into the groove on the base cabinet and set the dowels in place.

39 After finish sanding the entire dresser and jewelry box, apply a coat of red aniline, water-based dye. Wipe off the excess. The cabinet will look something like the project in this photo. It's a little shocking, especially to someone who might come through your shop at about this stage in the finishing process! Pay them no mind, because it's a work in progress.

40 After the dye is dry, apply a light-brown pigmented stain to the dresser and jewelry box. This will add depth to the color of the cabinet, and it should look like the project shown in this photo. Let the stain dry and apply two coats of sanding sealer. (Don't sand between the first and second coats because you could very easily sand into the stain.) After the second coat of sealer, lightly sand the sealer smooth, being very careful! Then apply three topcoats of finish. Use the light-brown pigmented stain to color the drawer fronts for both the dresser and the jewelry box. Finish these the same as the cabinets.

pine
DOUBLE LOUNGE

This project was copied from a photograph. It's the pioneer equivalent of our present-day futon. There are two frames made of alternating bed slats, and one frame can be pulled out to make a double bed. These double lounges were very popular in northeast America, Canada and Utah. Practicality was important to the early Mormon settlers, and these double lounges fit the bill. This lounge would originally have had a faux-grained finish, but I made this one out of pine and finished it with a light-brown stain and a topcoat of clear finish.

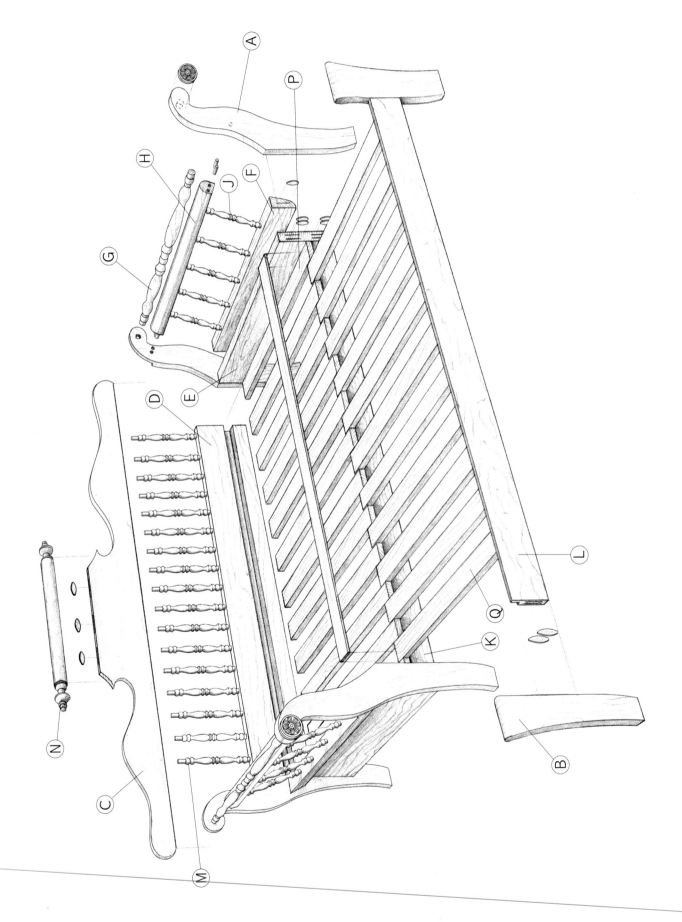

CUTTING LIST (INCHES) • pine double lounge

REF.	QTY.	PART	STOCK	THICKNESS	WIDTH	LENGTH	COMMENTS
A	4	Legs	Pine	$1\frac{1}{2}$	8	27	Two legs can be cut out of an 8x42 blank
B	2	Front Legs	Pine	$1\frac{1}{2}$	$4\frac{1}{2}$	14	
C	1	Top Back Rail	Pine	$1\frac{1}{2}$	$9\frac{1}{2}$	88	
D	1	Back Bottom Rail	Pine	$1\frac{1}{2}$	9	74	
E	2	Side Rails	Pine	$1\frac{1}{2}$	9	$26\frac{1}{2}$	
F	2	Side Spindle Rails	Pine	$1\frac{1}{2}$	$2\frac{3}{4}$	$26\frac{1}{2}$	
G	2	Arm Spindles	Pine	$1\frac{1}{2}$	$1\frac{1}{2}$	28	Turned to desired profile
H	2	Top Side Spindle Rails	Pine	$1\frac{1}{2}$	$1\frac{1}{2}$	$26\frac{1}{2}$	Attached with dowels
J	10	Side Spindles	Maple	1 dia.		8	Available at Woodworker's Supply
K	1	Inner Front Rail	Pine	$1\frac{1}{2}$	4	74	
L	1	Outer Front Rail	Pine	$1\frac{1}{2}$	$5\frac{1}{4}$	74	
M	17	Back Spindles	Maple	$\frac{7}{8}$ dia.		10	Available at Woodworker's Supply
N	1	Crest Finial	Pine	2 dia.		30	Turned with desired finial profile
P	12	Couch Base Slats	Pine	$1\frac{1}{4}$	3	28	
Q	11	Pullout Base Slats	Pine	$1\frac{1}{4}$	3	29	
R	1	Slat Connecting Rail	Oak	$\frac{3}{8}$	$2\frac{1}{2}$	$67\frac{1}{2}$	
S	2	Slat Guides	Pine	$\frac{1}{4}$+/.	$1\frac{1}{4}$	28	

CUTTING LIST (MILLIMETERS) • pine double lounge

REF.	QTY.	PART	STOCK	THICKNESS	WIDTH	LENGTH	COMMENTS
A	4	Legs	Pine	38	203	686	Two legs can be cut out of an 8x42 blank
B	2	Front Legs	Pine	38	115	356	
C	1	Top Back Rail	Pine	38	242	2235	
D	1	Back Bottom Rail	Pine	38	229	1880	
E	2	Side Rails	Pine	38	229	673	
F	2	Side Spindle Rails	Pine	38	70	673	
G	2	Arm Spindles	Pine	38	38	711	Turned to desired profile
H	2	Top Side Spindle Rails	Pine	38	38	673	Attached with dowels
J	10	Side Spindles	Maple	25 dia.		203	Available at Woodworker's Supply
K	1	Inner Front Rail	Pine	38	102	1880	
L	1	Outer Front Rail	Pine	38	133	1880	
M	17	Back Spindles	Maple	22 dia.		254	Available at Woodworker's Supply
N	1	Crest Finial	Pine	51 dia.		762	Turned with desired finial profile
P	12	Couch Base Slats	Pine	32	76	711	
Q	11	Pullout Base Slats	Pine	32	76	737	
R	1	Slat Connecting Rail	Oak	10	64	1715	
S	2	Slat Guides	Pine	6+/.	32	711	

PINE DOUBLE LOUNGE *continued*

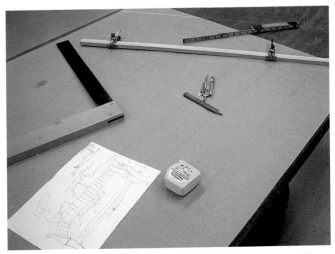

1 I recommend drawing a full-scale layout of this project. The project is symmetrical, so I drew just the right-half front elevation and an elevation end view. As you're drawing, things will become clear as to how it all fits together. In keeping with the spirit of the Mormon tradition of using what you have at hand, I thickness-glued the pine I had into 1½"-thick material. Sometimes I had to glue to width first, then to thickness. I had very little waste when I was finished with this project!

2 Make a template of the front leg out of ½" or ¾" plywood. Take your time making the curves flow smoothly into each other. Use the template as a guide and trace the shape of the legs onto the wood blanks. Also trace the bottom half of the leg onto the blanks for the two short front legs. Rough-cut all the legs, and use the template with a router and flush-trim bit to cut the legs to final shape. I screwed the template to the inside of each leg with two screws: one screw where the top turned arm is located and the other where the side rail is located. Be sure you're clear as to left and right, inside and outside. Mark the legs so you don't get confused.

3 On both sets of spindle rails (one top-and-bottom set for the left side and one for the right side), mark the proper spacing of the holes for the spindles. Drill the holes in the top spindle rails, then set the drill press table to the proper angle to drill the holes in the bottom spindle rails.

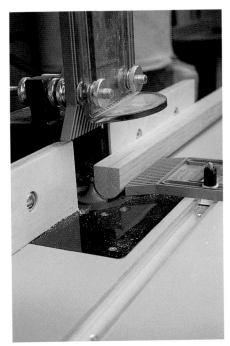

4 The top two edges of the top spindle side rails are then profiled with a ¾" roundover router bit.

5 Glue the bottom side spindle rail to the side rail. Make two of these assemblies.

6 I bought the side and back turned spindles ready-made (available from Woodworker's Supply or Woodcraft), but I needed to turn the two arm spindles. I traced the pattern of one of the back spindles onto a piece of paper and enlarged this on a copier until it was the size I needed to make a pattern for the arm (approximately 265 percent).

Mormon Pioneer Ingenuity

When members of the Church of Jesus Christ of Latter-day Saints (commonly known as Mormons) migrated west and settled in the Salt Lake valley, they had only what they brought with them. There were no trees (or anything else) in the valley. The Saints used the hardwood from their wagons to build furniture and cabinets. The Saints that followed were instructed to have their wagons and handcarts built to specification out of certain hardwoods: hickory for axle trees, red or slippery elm for hubs, white oak for spokes and wheel rims, white ash for fills or shafts and for making the cribs or beds that would hold all of the belongings to be moved. After the settlers arrived in Utah, the wagons and handcarts were disassembled and used to make cabinets and furniture.

The cabinetmakers that came to Utah brought with them the skills of their trade. They were influenced by English and Scandinavian styles. (Many of the settlers were from these countries.) Many cabinetmakers were skilled in the art of faux-graining. Furniture was made of pine harvested from the mountains and faux-grained to look like mahogany, oak and other more exotic woods. Brigham Young, the president of the Church at that time, was a master cabinetmaker and faux-graining artist. (For more information and step-by-step instructions on how to do faux-graining, see Bill Russell's book *Finishing Magic*, published by Popular Woodworking Books.)

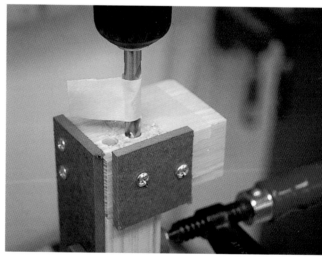

7 The ends of the top spindle rails are doweled to the legs on the end assemblies. The rails are too small to use a biscuit, so I used two ⅜" × 2" gluing dowels.

8 The turned arms are set into ⅞"-diameter by 1"-deep mortises in the legs. The two side rails and the back rail are attached to the legs with four large S-6 biscuits. S-6 biscuits are approximately $3^{5}/_{16}$" × $1^{3}/_{16}$" in size. With the biscuits doubled up, as shown by the slots in the photo, the strength of this joint is greatly increased. Cut the dado for the slats and drill the angled spindle holes in the back rail. Also drill the spindle holes in the crest rail at this time.

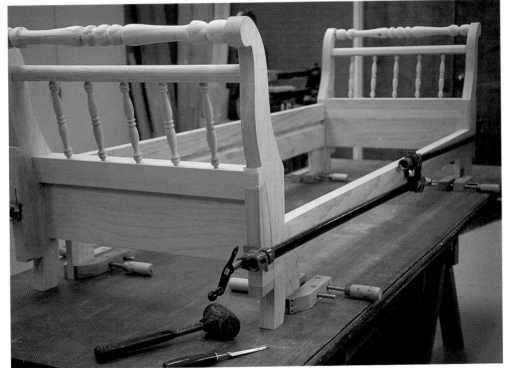

9 After the two ends of the lounge have been assembled, you might need an assistant to put the lounge assembly together. Note the four hand screws with scraps of wood clamped in them. These are holding the front and back rails to the correct height for assembling the lounge. (These legs helped my assistant and me have our hands free to get the clamps into place.)

10 Make a ¼" or ½" plywood template of the scrolling on the crest rail from the full-scale drawings. Trace around it onto the right half of the crest rail blank, and use a jigsaw to cut almost to the line (leaving about ⅛" of material on the outside of the line). Repeat for the left half of the crest rail. Clamp the template in place and rout the cut clean, using a flush-trim bit and a router. Repeat this on the other half of the crest rail. (I discovered it would be easier to drill the spindle holes in the crest rail before cutting the scrolls. See step 8.)

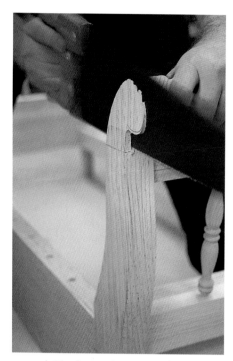

11 | Notches can be cut into the crest rail to match the profile of the top of the leg, or (and this is much easier) a notch can be cut into the top of the back leg.

12 | After fitting the leg notches to the crest rail, glue the crest rail to the back legs. Start at one leg and work your way down the lounge, inserting the spindles as you go.

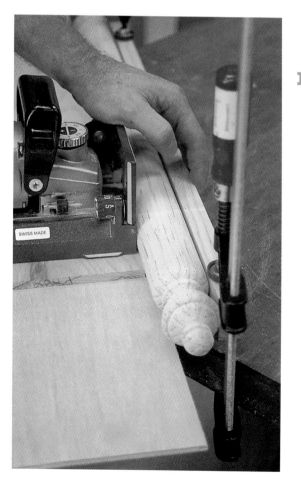

13 | I glued together the off-fall from the crest rail scroll cuts to make the turning blank for the crest rail finial. After turning the finial, I captured it between a strip of wood clamped to the assembly table and a piece of plywood. I adjusted the height of the cutter to cut three slots in the center of the diameter of the finial dowel. I then cut three matching slots in the top of the crest rail and glued the finial in place.

14 | Starting at one end of the lounge, install a slat against the side rail, in the dado in the back rail and the top of the front rail using glue and screws. Using two ¼" wood strips and an extra slat as spacers, locate the next slat and glue and screw it into place. Continue this process and install all the slats, making sure the final one is attached to the other end of the lounge.

15 | After assembling the front leg assembly, clamp it to the lounge and screw the slats to the front rail connecting the two short legs. (I visually centered these slats between the other slats on the lounge.) Then attach the slat connecting rail to the rear of the front leg assembly slats.

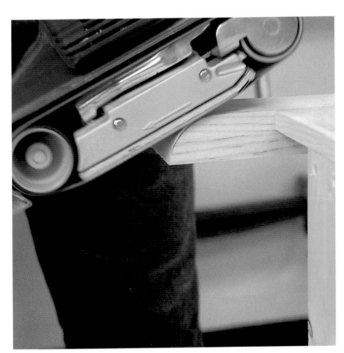

16 | Ease the tops of the short front legs using the belt sander. This roundover softens the look of these front legs and helps them visually flow into the tall front legs.

17 | If you like, glue a decorative, carved disk at the top of the front legs.

resources and suppliers

Ball and Ball
Exton, Pennsylvania
(800) 257-3711
www.ballandball-us.com
Hardware reproductions.

Horton Brasses Inc.
Cromwell, Connecticut
(800) 754-9127
www.horton-brasses.com
Hardware for antique furniture. Hepple-white, Chippendale and Victorian brass hardware. Hand forged iron hardware.

Constantine's
Bronx, New York
(800) 223-8087
Probably the oldest woodworking company in the country (176 years). Wide selection of tools, woods, veneers and hardware.

Lee Valley Tools Ltd.
Ogdensburg, New York
(800) 871-8158
www.leevalley.com
Fine woodworking tools and hardware. They have everything from instrument-maker's to log builder's hand tools. They design and manufacture many quality tools under the VERITAS label.

Rockler Woodworking and Hardware
Medina, Minnesota
(800) 279-4441
www.rockler.com
Woodworking tools and hardware.

Sikkens Decorative Wood Finishes
Troy, Michigan
(800) 833-7288
www.sikkens.com
Wood finishes.

Van Dyke's Restorers
Woonsocket, South Dakota
(800) 558-1234
Supplies for Upholstery and Antique Restoration. Antique reproduction hardware.

Wolfcraft Inc.
Itasca, Illinois
(630) 773-4777
www.wolfcraft.com
Woodworking hardware.

Woodcraft Supply Corp.
Parkersburg, West Virginia
(800) 225-1153
www.woodcraft.com
Woodworking hardware.

Woodworker's Hardware
Sauk Rapids, Minnesota
(800) 383-0130
www.wwhardware.com
Woodworking hardware.

Woodworker's Supply
Casper, Wyoming
(800) 645-9292
Woodworking tools and accessories, finishing supplies, books and plans.

index